LUCRETIUS AND THE BAT WITH BLUE EYES

LUCRETIUS AND THE BAT WITH BLUE EYES

EXPLAINING THE UNIVERSE WITH THE ALPHABET

ANDREA MORO

THE MIT PRESS
CAMBRIDGE, MASSACHUSETTS
LONDON, ENGLAND

The MIT Press
Massachusetts Institute of Technology
77 Massachusetts Avenue, Cambridge, MA 02139
mitpress.mit.edu

Published by arrangement with The Italian Literary Agency.

The MIT Press would like to thank the anonymous peer reviewers who provided
comments on drafts of this book. The generous work of academic experts
is essential for establishing the authority and quality of our publications. We
acknowledge with gratitude the contributions of these otherwise uncredited readers.

This book was set in PF DinText Pro by New Best-set Typesetters Ltd. Printed and
bound in the United States of America.

Library of Congress Cataloging-in-Publication Data

Names: Moro, Andrea author
Title: Lucretius and the bat with blue eyes : explaining the universe with the alphabet /
    Andrea Moro.
Description: Cambridge, Massachusetts : The MIT Press, 2025. | Includes
    bibliographical references and index.
Identifiers: LCCN 2025000334 (print) | LCCN 2025000335 (ebook) |
    ISBN 9780262554015 paperback | ISBN 9780262385657 epub |
    ISBN 9780262385664 pdf
Subjects: LCSH: Lucretius Carus, Titus—Language | Lucretius Carus, Titus. De
    rerum natura | LCGFT: Literary criticism
Classification: LCC PA6495 .M67 2025 (print) | LCC PA6495 (ebook) | DDC 187—
    dc23/eng/20250519
LC record available at https://lccn.loc.gov/2025000334
LC ebook record available at https://lccn.loc.gov/2025000335

10   9   8   7   6   5   4   3   2   1

EU Authorised Representative: Easy Access System Europe, Mustamäe tee 50,
10621 Tallinn, Estonia | Email: gpsr.requests@easproject.com

You must always be ready to give an explanation to everyone who asks you for the reason for the hope that is in you.

—1 Peter 3:15

CONTENTS

PROLOGUE: A GLASS WITH WATER AND ICE, AND A NOTE *PRO DOMO MEA*

I'm sitting at my desk, a glass of water with two ice cubes and a book before me. Sitting on the other side of the desk is a little girl: Federica, my niece. She has just learned to read; she is very curious, like her younger brother Marco, and she is waiting for my answer in silence. We often play together: Sometimes we pretend to be crazy cooks. We verbally invent disgusting recipes that involve good ingredients, such as a coffee and anchovy shake; sometimes we carry out simple experiments. Yesterday, I showed her the cupped part of a teaspoon after I'd stirred my tea with it and asked her to look at her reflection in it. Then, holding the spoon halfway up the handle, I rotated it with my fingers so that she was looking at its concave side: she stared at it bewildered. She saw her reflection was now upside down and thought I had performed a trick. She asked for the teaspoon and for a while didn't speak, inspecting it carefully.

Just now she asked me what water and ice are made of. I tell her that they are made of the same thing: Both are water, but when water gets very cold it becomes very hard and you can even shape it; you just have to put it in an empty mold when it is less cold and it will take on that shape, or you can carve it using the tools a sculptor would use with marble. She seems convinced. Then she asks me if glass is also like ice since the two look so much alike. I answer no, but she seems less convinced. She tells me that maybe if the glass gets very hot it becomes like water. "I'd be tempted to agree with you," I reply, "but I can't tell you they're made of the same thing." I try to change the subject. She asks me if every different thing is made of something different: If a desk is made of a desk, clouds of clouds. She's set me up. I'm not the first to have been cornered by this question: It's one that has tormented many people. There is something disturbing in the thought that every object is made of something totally different from any other object: the glass, the ice, the table, the book, the room, along with all the other objects the latter contains, and of course the room itself. This disturbing thought is due not so much to the fact that there seem to be an infinite number of types of things—many things in nature seem to be endless, like the stars, for example—but to the fact that when faced with things made of the same material—a wooden table and a wooden chair, for example—we regard them as if they are made of something different; as if there existed a *tablehood* and a *chairness* inherent to them.

Of course, I know that's not the case, because I know what atoms are, and even if I've never worked on them, I trust those who tell me that all the things I see are made up of almost a hundred different kinds of atoms—some of them very rare, some less so, and others very abundant—and these come together in precise compositions to give rise to elements such as hydrogen, which is in water, ice, and the sun. But how do I tell my niece this, let alone explain it to her? And what is an explanation in the first place? How does an explanation differ from a fairy tale or a legend? I obviously can't discuss quantum theory and experimental physics with Federica. If I want to explain to her that the world is a combination of very few kinds of particles that obey four fundamental forces, I'll need to convince her that all things—whether similar like water and oil, or as different as iron is to a stone and custard, or water is to a glass— are made of a few ingredients, and it's the different ways they combine that make them different.

Absorbed by these thoughts, I open the book on my desk. I'd had no intention of reading it; it's there only because I wanted to move it from a collection of Latin texts to the shelf holding my favorite books. It is a used and underlined copy of Lucretius's *De Rerum Natura*: a classic. Sure, it's easy to say "classic." There are words that have settled into our personal dictionaries—the ones we carry in our heads— which have stopped generating wonder, words we think of the same way we think of a friend's name when we run into them. Words that for this very reason we should inspect now and then, either to scrape off the sediment of time, or to resharpen the edges that usage has blunted. We hardly notice them, anesthetized as we are by habit, until someone asks us to explain them and all at once these words come back to life and dart away, so charged with new life that one loses one's grip on them. One such word is *classic*.

In one of his famous texts, Italo Calvino taught us what a classic is in an innovative, fascinating, comprehensive way.[1] For our purposes we just need to establish three of its components, synthetically: First, a classic is a voice that conveys something different to everyone, but it is something that is always of import; second, a classic is a voice that speaks even if one listens to only some of what it has to say; third—if we may be so bold as to add to Calvino's definition—a classic is a voice that teaches you to ask questions that are newer than those it has already addressed.

So, what you will find here is what Lucretius says to me, two thousand years after he first spoke, how he enables me to respond to new ideas I have learned from others and, above all, to new questions that I have formulated (sometimes with others). What you will find in what follows is the impact of a genius who, in order to make people understand what the world is made of, relied on what we all understand language to be made of—that which is deeply familiar to us and yet remains even more mysteriously unknown. This powerful analogy—the structure of language as a guide for understanding the structure of the world—is, like all analogies, the ultimate goal of science: an explanation that allows everyone to see the hidden side of the tapestry that we perceive with our senses, by building analogies between facts that seem completely unrelated and, in doing so, simplifying our understanding of the world with respect to how it appears to us. We can't be sure if this grammatical view of the world really explains the world, but it certainly explains how we see it.

But there is one other thing that a classic will give a reader, and it is perhaps what experience in general also sometimes provides: something that can arise without being forced or imagined—the unexpected. It is precisely what you cannot foresee that will increase your knowledge of the world and of yourself; everything else is just deductions from premises, important as they may be. And in reading Lucretius, hunting for passages that could explain the world with the alphabet and grammar, I became aware of two intuitions on his part that, in an absolutely unexpected way, correlate with the most modern understanding of human language.

The first intuition concerns the existence of "impossible languages," a discovery that brought about a radical change in perspective in contemporary linguistics and had resulted from decades of formal and comparative analyses of languages and then experimentally proven by some experiments in the neurobiology of language.[2] It is the one discovery that more than any other allows us to ask the right questions about our species, our origin, and our (eventual) destination. It is also what allows us to understand how we are unique compared to all other animals, and even compared to machines. These matters were already implicit in Lucretius's text.

The second intuition Lucretius had was the idea that languages were not born as the result of a need, the same way that ears, our human ears, did not sprout from our head due to the need to hear. Organs do satisfy a need, but they were not born out of the need they satisfy. In fact, the opposite is true. Lucretius understood this, and with this understanding he investigated the origin of language. Not everything is always clear and coherent in his text, but what is significant is that he thought of language in this novel and wonderful way, and that in doing so he continues to stimulate us.

These are at least two ways that *De Rerum Natura* still speaks to us; my goal here is only to underline its text in pencil, so to speak, and write a few notes in the margin—to share the extraordinary experience of reading this text and to encourage the formulation of new questions. An experience that came to me as I tried to answer a little girl.

I

LANGUAGE AS A TOOL, OR TO EXPLAIN THE WORLD WITH THE ALPHABET

Let's start from scratch: It won't take long, but an explanation is necessary. The world is made of atoms. To explain such a thing, however, one must first explain what it means to "explain." *Explain*: *ex*, meaning "out," combined with *planus*, meaning "flat"—to make level, or flatten out. A beautiful image, common to many languages. Take a fabric, perhaps with a printed design, or a crumpled-up sheet of paper containing a text, and spread it out on a surface so that it is completely flat and its full content is visible, without any creases. The same thing is said of the sails of a boat that swell out when you want to get the most out of them, so that the wind will move you and get you to a different place. This is how *explain* came to mean "describe in an understandable way" a question that seems complex to us—to make it completely open and visible, unfolded, without (conceptual) creases.

But when you shift from metaphorical fabric to reality, it's not always clear what an explanation calls for. Sometimes one can simply list the parts of an object, or outline the relationships between the parts of a concept, but this is not always enough. Lucretius knows this and convinces us with an example. It seems simple enough, but Lucretius asks himself a question that even modern physicists find difficult. Even the relatively neglected nineteenth-century biologist Emil Du Bois-Reymond thought it was a question that could not be answered.[1] Lucretius wonders if there is a way to explain how objects move—or rather, if their movements can be explained in a simple way. The question is particularly deceptive because our senses immediately perceive two types of movements; flames, for example, rise upward while stones fall downward. Not many people notice these two divergent movements or ask why flames are subject to different forces than stones, but Lucretius does. This question was all the more important in his time because there were still those who believed, based on Aristotle's notes on physics, that different types of objects followed their own specific nature in their movements, the way a lover follows after the one they love, as Aristotle metaphorically put it. Therefore, natural attraction leads stones to fall to the ground and flames to rise up. But Lucretius wants to use this example to make it clear that this theory explains nothing. If there are two movements, one upward and one downward, and we posit that there are two forces determining them, we gain nothing: Two different movements explained by assuming two different forces remain just as complex as before such an explanation. Lucretius wants us to understand what an explanation must consist of if it is to work, and offers striking examples involving flames and blood:

> I believe that now the time has come to confirm
> this fact: that no material object
> can move or move upward by means of its own force.
> Don't be fooled by bodies of flame
> because they are generated and grow upward;
> even the wonderful ears of corn grow upward, and so do the trees;
> but bodies, due to their weight, always move downward.
> And even when fires leap up to the roofs of houses

and with their flame rapidly devour planks and beams,

believe not that they do so spontaneously, with no force pushing from below.

Similarly, the blood from our body spurts

outward and upward, spreading red everywhere.

Can you not see how hard water repels

boards and beams? The more we push them down

and force them to the bottom,

the more forcefully it throws them back up,

rejected, so that more than half their length emerges and jumps out.

Yet we do not doubt that these things, because of what they are made,

are all carried down through the void.

So, too, must flames must rise upward, once compressed by the air, even if

whatever weight they have struggles to draw them downward.[2]

Lucretius is telling us, in summary, that for an explanation to be an explanation, it must contain fewer principles than the phenomenon it wants to explain. His example is clear: Everything falls downward; only one force acts on everything, but various objects, including flames and blood, move in different directions depending on the density of the substance in which they are immersed. On the other hand, if I hold, say, a soccer ball tightly in my hands and let it go, it will fall downward if I am standing in the open air; but if I am standing at the bottom of a swimming pool filled with water, it will rise upward to the surface. There is no need to think of two opposing forces acting on the ball. The direction of movement depends on the density of the medium: Water pushes the ball and the air it contains up because it is lighter than water, whereas air is compressed by the weight of the ball (and the air contained in it) and pushes the ball down. Here then is what an explanation requires: It must stipulate principles that are fewer in number than the observed phenomenon. In other words, the theory must be less complicated than what is observed; otherwise, it will lead to what happens to those who want to include every detail in a map—the well-known paradox of the map that must contain a small map, which must itself contain a small map, and so on ad infinitum. In short, we end up with the paradox of not so much a useless map but an impossible map.[3] Leaving aside the notion of a map of a map, the fact remains that when we commission a map, we must always specify what needs to be highlighted for a specific region: the altitude of mountains, or the distribution of population, or even the average rainfall in summer. This is what we must always keep in mind: Any explanation has to be less complicated than what is observed, and it must respond to a specific and explicit request for knowledge. There are no universal explanations.

Now we can return to trying to understand how Lucretius explained the world and how I can do so for my niece, hoping to have eliminated tablehood, chairness, and the like.

1 TO DECOMPOSE

I now return to the glass of water with ice and the avalanche of questions that observing it generated. I decided to agree with Lucretius on the matter; I can't not agree with Lucretius. The first concept to understand is that things are not made up of different things; but for this to be possible we must also realize that things can be composed of common elements. That requires an "atomic" vision of reality, where "atomic" derives etymologically from the ancient Greek prefix *a-* (in-) and the root of the verb *temno* (divide): indivisible (objects). Lucretius had adopted such a vision after studying a theory of Democritus, a physicist born in Greece just over three and a half centuries before him. It was a theory that took strong hold: not only of other physicists but also of philosophers, such as the great Epicurus to whom Lucretius dedicated his poem. Lucretius believed in it, but the problem for him was to enable those who had not studied physics to understand the depth, power, necessity, and even beauty of this theory. But how to do so? Lucretius had a stroke of genius: We already know of something that is made up of smaller elements which cannot be further divided and doesn't call for experiments and sophisticated technology to be easily understandable. You yourself have it before your eyes: words. And Lucretius tells us this:

It is better to think that many corpuscles exist and that many things

are made of them, the way letters of the alphabet make words,

than think there can be things not made of primitive elements.[1]

This is the source of Lucretius's illumination, and it is this spark that will cast light on everything: The world of things is composed the way the world of words is. Lucretius does not offer us certainty—doing so is not possible—but he offers us a parallel world in which things work in a similar manner and makes it credible. There are no things that are not made of smaller things that, in a certain sense, came into existence before them: the first, primitive elements. Similarly, there are no words that are not made of letters and the letters exist before the words themselves. Otherwise, it would be as if every word were made of completely distinct sounds chosen from a fixed, limited repertoire—in simpler terms, an alphabet—which would be completely exhausted very rapidly. Such a language is not *logically* impossible, but if this were so it would be useless, for there would exist very few different words (which is obviously never the case in human languages), just as in the realm of physics there would be very few different things.

It is also interesting to note that Lucretius gives different names to the primitive elements of which things are made and the elements of which words are made: "corpuscles" (*corpora*) for the former, "elements" (*elementa*) for the latter. No one knows for sure where the second word

CHAPTER 1

comes from, but we know it was also used as a grammatical term. The life of words is strange: The term that Lucretius takes from grammar to compare it to the corpuscles of which things are made (*elements*) in modern languages stands precisely for the name of things—the name of the things from which things are made when they can no longer be reduced to other things. While today we know of almost a hundred different natural types of elements, for many centuries there were considered to be of only four fundamental types: water, air, earth, and fire.

We have accepted that things are all made up of smaller and more primitive things; but where does that leave us? Are we to believe that everything is just a shapeless bag holding smaller things? Lucretius immediately corrects this potential assumption: What matters is not only which elements, which corpuscles, make up things—the relationship between these elements is fundamental. It is important to remember that Lucretius believed that if things are composed of corpuscles, corpuscles themselves move, as Democritus claimed. To Democritus, movement served to demonstrate that the world was not some kind of huge block of marble, or a colossal crystal, fixed once and forevermore. Movement allowed for and ensured that change could take place—although Plato, for example, rejected this explanation, because it did not account for the reproduction of harmonious and similar organizations of elements (that is, the reproduction of things and animals). Moreover, which is of no small importance, this theory also allowed for the unexpected, because in moving, elements always end up colliding and producing new combinations. Let's hear what Lucretius has to say about it:

> And often, with the primitive elements, it is of great import
>
> what other elements they combine with and in what position
>
> and which among them give and receive movement;
>
> for they are the same exact elements that make up sky and sea, land, rivers, and sun;
>
> the same that constitute cornfields and trees and all living beings.
>
> But they mix with each other and move in different ways.
>
> Indeed, in these very verses we see that many letters
>
> are the same in many words,
>
> yet it must be admitted that these verses and words
>
> differ both in meaning and in sound, the medium in which they are expressed.
>
> So powerful are letters even when their order alone is permuted.[2]

One couldn't be more explicit. Position matters, and it matters a lot; indeed, the position of elements is as important in things as it is for letters in words. I can pronounce the word "wand," recombine the eight letters, and obtain another one: "dawn"—the same letters in different positions produce completely different meanings. So what prevents us from thinking that this also happens in the world of things, where it is corpuscles rather than letters changing position? Lucretius's words are true conceptual dynamite due to their explanatory power, clarity, and synthesis: *even when their order alone is permuted* (*permutato ordine solo*, in Latin), Lucretius tells us, and this is the heart of atomic theory and how Lucretius takes one step further in spreading and strengthening the explanation of how the universe is made. It's not just the ingredients that matter, but how each ingredient is related to the others—that is, to the overall structure. The simplest relation of all, the one with which Lucretius begins, is therefore the relation of linear order: permutation of the order alone can change everything, he tells us.

And the analogy with words allows Lucretius to refine the idea of the recombination of letters, and therefore of corpuscles, by showing that it is not necessary to change everything to have different objects, be it a thing or a word. Even minimal changes may be enough:

> So now don't you see that [. . .]
> the same elements, slightly exchanged,
> create fire and wood? And in this identical way,
> words themselves are created by slightly exchanging
> their letters, to express the distinct words *ligna* [wood]
> and *ignes* [fire].[3]

The Latin pun is evident: *ligna*, which means "wood," has almost all the same letters as *ignes*, which means "fire"; one transforms into the other by changing the *a* to *e* and replacing the *s* with an *l*. Similarly, it doesn't take much to transform wood into fire: Just a spark and the transformation is complete. Another symmetry between the domain of words and things is thus established through reference to common experience alone.

Then, Lucretius takes a step back, if only a small one. He has just convinced us that things are made of corpuscles the same way that words are made of letters, but he doesn't want us to take this to simply mean that everything is made of the same things. There is a difference between the basic components of words and those of things, and it is a significant one:

> Looking here and there in our own verses, we see
>
> that many letters are common to many words:
>
> yet it must be recognized that verses and words
>
> are made up of different letters.
>
> I am not saying that the same few letters occur in every word
>
> or that no two words are made up of identical letters
>
> but that in general not all words are made of the same letters as others.[4]

The time has come for a summary. Lucretius provides one without too many shortcuts by looking at the nearest material, namely his own text:

> Even in our own verses it is important
>
> that each letter is placed in a certain position and order;
>
> the same letters mean "sky," "sea," "lands," "rivers," "the sun";
>
> the same ones mean "harvest," "trees," "living beings";
>
> most, if not all, of the letters are similar to each other;

but it is their position that makes the meanings different. Likewise, with regard to things themselves, when distances, paths, connections, weights, impacts, common trajectories, positions, the configurations of matter change,
the things themselves must consequently change.[5]

There is no need to summarize his summary; it is enough for us to note that as Lucretius moves from words to things, he is starting to specify what counts, the way he specified that for the letters of the alphabet their position counts. With things, on the other hand, more complex spatial measurements than linear position are in play: distances, paths, connections. If these change, then the things also change. As with the example of the alphabet, this decomposition of reality into corpuscles can no longer be accused of being magic.

Let's stop for a moment and think about those born two millennia after Lucretius. An initial, naive, question arises: Who has read Lucretius over the centuries? Who has brought his intuitions and images to fruition? The answer doesn't seem obvious to me. Let's start with the question of language. Obviously, I am referring to the moment at which Lucretius's text became available again, that is, at the beginning of the fifteenth century when Poggio Bracciolini discovered it. The legendary humanist recovered a copy of the manuscript from the abbey of San Gallo in Switzerland, not surprisingly founded by a disciple of San Colombano, an Irish monk to whom we owe the preservation of the core of Latin literature at the abbey of Bobbio in Northern Italy during the Longobard era. Since then, *De Rerum Natura* has been regrafted onto the impressive tree of Western literature. I won't go any further in this adventurous and exciting story:[6] I only wish to reflect on the impact this text has had in the modern and contemporary era, specifically with respect to Lucretius's perspective on language.

The passages by Lucretius quoted above are interesting not only because they offer a way for people to understand the atomic structure of reality; they are also interesting from a linguistic point of view. The decomposition of all words into common letters, the role position plays for each letter, the fact that a minimal change in a word's pronunciation is enough to change its meaning—these intuitions remind us of the foundations of one of the two fundamental revolutions in contemporary linguistics: that of structuralism, the result of Ferdinand de Saussure's reflections in Geneva in the early 1900s. Saussure was fond of comparing a grammar to the situation of an ongoing chess game: It is useless to know where, say, the black queen is if we do not know what other pawns are in play. In a *système* (which was later called "structure"), on the other hand, the reciprocal positions of all the elements count. Not only that: It doesn't even matter what the pieces are made of; if the black queen shatters and is replaced by a red ripe strawberry, you can continue playing, unless there are other similar strawberries on the board; the strawberry holds as long as it stands out from the other pieces, the same way the queen did. Saussure, in a crucial passage for the history of linguistics, said as much, dropping on us, with the first sentence of the following quotation, a kind of epistemological bomb with incalculable effects:

> In language there are only differences. Even more important: a difference generally implies positive terms between which the difference is set up; but in language there are only differences *without positive terms*. Whether we take the signified or the signifier, language has neither ideas nor sounds that existed before the linguistic system, but only conceptual and phonic differences that have issued from the system.[7]

Saussure praises difference as a structuring element. This vision is so powerful that structuralism, born in linguistics, spread as a global vision over the last century to many domains. It characterized all the scientific and artistic reflections elaborated in this period, from architecture to biology, music to psychology, anthropology to literature, mathematics to painting, and including, obviously, linguistics—so much so that one could arguably refer to that century in its entirety as being the age of Structuralism, just as we refer to its immediately preceding ones as being the Baroque age, or the age of Romanticism or the Enlightenment. Lucretius grasped the value of the structural relationship in his text and delivered it to us like a message in a bottle that took two millennia to finally land on the desk of a Geneva professor.

Nevertheless, in addition to its relevance for thinking about language, Lucretius's text also offers a model for understanding reality in general—something all too relevant today, as a useless battle is being resumed that had already seemed resolved in the middle of the last century.[8] But here I just want to highlight how Lucretius's text demonstrates how the classics can act as a stimulus to finding new connections and reawakening dormant reflections. Everyone will receive a different impression, of course. It's like when you go on a trip: Even if you go to the same place as others, you come back with photographs that won't be identical to theirs. I took two such personal mental snapshots and want to tell you about them.

The first comes from Plato. It concerns the way we understand the world and also starts from a linguistic example. I take language to be like the night sky: Both have always been the same for humans with only irrelevant differences over time, but they have always given rise to new, sometimes incompatible reflections. My first snapshot is a couple of sentences taken from *Theaetetus*. Plato is reflecting on what a syllable is in relation to the sounds that compose it. It is not an easy text, but the basic problem is nevertheless evident and concerns our ability to recognize reality in general:

> Single letters are unknowable, yet syllables are knowable. . . . Perhaps we should consider that the syllable is not just the letters, but a single concept that has arisen from them, with a single form of its own, different from the letters.[9]

Plato here speaks of "single letters" (my translation of *stoicheia*, which corresponds to the Latin *elementa*) and of "syllables," which literally means "(things) taken together," or "compounds," as translated from Latin. The intuition expressed here poses an unresolved dilemma, not only by Plato but also today by both neuroscience and philosophy. How do we understand something that is made up of parts: by locating the parts and putting them together in the mind later, or by knowing the whole and then breaking it down? Once again the parallel with language is clear and effective, even at levels higher than that of the syllable. If, for example, I hear the word "reusable," do I break the word down into *re-*, *use*, and *-able* to understand "something that can be used again," or do I understand the total meaning and then, perhaps with a little effort, break the word down into those bricks of meaning that linguists call "morphemes"? After all, in English we do not break a word like *react* in the same way and interpret is as if it were *re-act*, as meaning "act again." One could even radicalize the question and ask: Which came first, the morpheme or the word? In a language, do individual sounds even exist, or just syllables? There is no single answer. I have come to the conclusion that we can say that something exists if and only if it plays a role in an explanation, be it a physical object or a new type of number for solving an equation. I don't know if that's convincing, but it certainly doesn't convince me to say that only what I can touch or smell or see or hear or taste exists. Which brings us to my second mental photograph.

This time it is from a physicist, so let's return to the world of things, though this is precisely why the quote is surprising. We are used to imagining science as the domain of observing what exists, but the more one delves into the scientific method the more one realizes that this naive vision is wrong, even in the modern era. We all take for granted that experiments are at the heart of science; the term *experiment* obviously alludes to experience, and the reproducibility of results under the same conditions is the fulcrum of the scientific method, but experience is only a mediator for understanding deeper and inaccessible facts than the experience itself. To understand this thought, it is useful to refer to an exchange between Salviati and Simplicio from Galileo's *Dialogue Concerning the Two Chief World Systems*:

> Salviati: . . . But tell me: if you have a flat surface, as polished as a mirror and of substance as hard as steel, and which was not parallel to the horizon, but somewhat inclined, and you placed a perfectly spherical ball upon it, one made of a heavy and very hard material such as, for example, bronze, what do you think it would do when released? Don't you believe (as I do) that it would stand still? . . .

> Simplicio: I understood everything very well, and to your question I answer that it would continue to move *indefinitely*, if the inclination of the plane lasted long enough, and with continuously accelerated movement; for such is the nature of the heavy bodies: they gain strength in movement, and the greater the declivity, the greater the velocity will be.

Galilei, who regarded experimentation and experience as being the foundation of the scientific method, here speaks of the infinite ("move *indefinitely*," he says): precisely something that no human being can ever experience and an experiment that no one can undertake, be it a question of formal infinity (such as that of numbers) or physical infinity (such as that of measurement). This allows us to understand that science, although it must go through experience, may reach an explanation of what is accessible to the senses by resorting to hypotheses that do not derive from direct sensory experience (such as the notion of infinite). Doing so, however, requires a powerful razor to shear away magical interpretations of reality and not allow us to fall back into the delusions of alchemy; this razor itself plays a role in the explanation. If this criterion for existence—what exists is what plays a role in explanation—is considered unjustified, we may at least accept the weaker position of the physicist Jean-Baptiste Perrin, who claimed that the task of science is to "explain what is visible and complicated with what is simple and invisible."[10] It surely is an illuminating statement, but also one that could be seen as the germination of the seeds Lucretius had planted two millennia earlier.

Lucretius explained to us how things are broken down into corpuscles and words are broken down into letters, but in doing so he raised a new, necessary, and important question: How do these primitive elements we have hypothesized combine with each other? The first principle is that of heterogeneity, which was the prime mover that led us to suppose the existence of corpuscles in the first place:

> No thing whose nature is visible to the naked eye
> consists of a single kind of primitive element
> and there is nothing not made of mixed primitive elements.[1]

Lucretius doesn't say as much, but we can now construct an example for ourselves using words. Except for those rare cases of words made up of a single letter and certain conjunctions or interjections, words made up of several letters are composed of different letters. Once again, the worlds—the world of things and the world of words—are parallel.

Then Lucretius addresses primitive elements in a more analytical way. He begins by asking himself quantitative questions, wondering how many primitive elements there are, but without confusing the number of copies with the number of original types. First, we clarify the number of copies of primitive elements:

. . . the primitive elements

of which things are made, which are similar to each other,

are infinite.[2]

They are infinite: It could not be clearer. We have the same clarity for primitive element types:

. . . the primitive elements of things

exist in a limited modality of forms.[3]

Here, without question, is Lucretius's genius: Although the number of copies of primitive elements (atoms, seeds, or corpuscles, as you like) is infinite, the number of types is not. In a very clear way, Lucretius is referencing the spatial dimension of things, their shape. Again, the analogy to the alphabet holds: For example, there are an infinite number of copies of each vowel but only a limited number of vowel types. His awareness of the power of the analysis of words and language in terms of primitive elements is such that it seems the language model was his guide for imagining the world model, rather than the other way around. In fact, there are really no compelling reasons for thinking that the types of primitive elements, not just the number of their copies, are infinite.

When speaking of infinity, of course, mathematics also comes to mind: There, too, are finite digits and infinite numbers, but at the time of Lucretius, the wonderful ideas Fibonacci imported into the West from the Arab world— along with any formal thinking in terms of infinities and numbers—was uncomfortable for the Latins, who must have needed refined calculations to build the monuments that we still admire today, which they carried out with square and compass—which is to say with geometry and not with numbers.

In sum, Lucretius manages to grasp the fact that the things of the world, which apparently differ from each other, are made up of a limited number of types of primitive elements that are found in the world in an unlimited number of copies.

Lucretius must now turn to a different though strictly related issue: namely, to explain the force behind the assembly of these primitive elements, which in themselves could just stay isolated and disorganized. Here the theory of Democritus, adopted by Epicurus, becomes fundamental. The motor of the organization consists in the random movements (the *parénklisis* in Greek, or *clināmen* in Latin, which mean "motion with an inclined direction") to which the corpuscles are subjected. Talking about movement in those remote times, however, was not at all obvious. With Aristotle, according to whom things would stand still once they reached their final destination (something dropping to the floor, for example), it was not easy to explain why, if you throw a stone against a wall, it still moves in the air after it has detached from your hand. For Aristotle, there must be a force that continues to push it. He ingeniously thought that the air in front of the stone violently moved behind the stone and that this somehow made the stone move forward. Had there been a vacuum—thought Aristotle—the stone would not have been able to move. Physicists of all ages have confronted each other over this story of emptiness and movement, even today: From Descartes's theories of vortices to Newton's shift from causal search to predictions, from Albert Einstein's reduction of gravity to a distortion of the space-time four-dimensional metric to the conflict between gravitational fields and quantum theory in the hunt for the (mythical) particle mediating gravity (the graviton).[4] Maybe Emil Du Bois-Reymond was in fact right in admitting that what causes things to move will forever remain a mystery. But for our purposes, we'll leave aside the two thousand years between Lucretius and us, as well as the three centuries between Aristotle and Lucretius (and those between Democritus and Aristotle). In short, we'll restrict ourselves to reading Lucretius. And here, the analogy with language falls apart: There is apparently nothing among the letters of the alphabet analogous to movement. More generally, the problem is raised here as to what we can understand of the whole world: Can we grasp it in its entirety? Can we access all its invariant laws? Lucretius is illuminating also with respect to this specific problem. Witness the following passage where he tries to prove the existence of chaotic movement:

> In fact, look carefully every time the sun's rays
> slip into dark houses and spread their light;
> you'll see in empty space many corpuscles mix
> in many ways in the light of the rays
> and engage in scuffles and battles as in an eternal
> duel, fighting endlessly in ranks

in continuous aggregation and disintegration without
  cease;

from this you can hypothesize how it happens in immense
  space

that the primitive elements of which things are made are
  continually thrown.

And so a small phenomenon can offer the image

of greater events and a pathway to knowledge.[5]

This is an absolute gem. After a piece of pure poetry in which Lucretius sings of dust crossed by light and turns it into an epic, he provides—on a gnoseological, epistemological, and heuristic level—an invaluable clue as to what we need to understand when we try to understand the world in general and not just movement in particular: that to understand the whole, we must necessarily follow the path traced out by our understanding of a particular. We must keep this gem in mind when approaching this (and many other issues) presented in Lucretius's poem.

Indeed, the idea of order being generated through chaotic movement is perhaps the weakest part of Democritus's theory and, therefore, of what Lucretius wishes to communicate. There's not much to add to it in terms of content, but we should note one extremely interesting fact. A major authority, contemporary with Lucretius himself, took issue with this theory based on random movement or chaos, and his doing so was all the more unexpected since it was precisely the same person who wanted to see this poem into publication and who agreed with his brother that it was filled with not only great flashes of the imagination but also much literary talent—an authority who dictated the law in Rome and changed its political and cultural structure for many centuries to come: Marcus Tullius Cicero. His argument against the idea of chaos as the origin of order unexpectedly returns us to a linguistic model, as if movement, excluded in language, were rendered implausible precisely by thinking of the order of language itself. Cicero says:

> At this point should I not be surprised that anyone would believe that solid and indivisible bodies, carried along by the force of their weight by virtue of their completely casual contact, build the world in all its beauty and richness? I see no reason why anyone willing to admit that this could be so shouldn't also think that, if one took together a great number of copies of the same shape of the twenty-one letters of the alphabet, built in gold or some other material, and threw them onto the ground, that they would offer up the complete *Annales* of Ennius, ready to be read. I doubt whether chance would be able to provide so much as a single verse.[6]

Cicero presents the order of the entire world—the cosmos, even—through the order of the letters of the alphabet in a text. We need to face a complicated fact: Cicero, who takes a stand against the theory of Democritus, which was also the inspiration for Lucretius's beloved poem, uses the same powerful and incisive metaphor based on language that Lucretius himself had used to demonstrate his own opposite thesis. It is a paradox on more than one level, but not a surprising one.

In fact, we are faced with a fundamental conflict that has never been completely resolved over the centuries: Where does the order we experience in our lives come from, if everything is made up of corpuscles moving chaotically? In this regard, an assumption has become common, sometimes referred to as the "butterfly effect"—the idea that small changes in a very complex system can have large chaotic consequences. For example, a book by Fred Hoyle, *The Intelligent Universe*, includes a quote from the prestigious magazine *Nature* that makes a comparison that parallels the one by Cicero: "A junkyard contains all the bits and pieces of a Boeing 747, dismembered and in disarray. A whirlwind happens to blow through the yard. What is the chance that after its passage a fully assembled 747, ready to fly, will be found standing there? So small as to be negligible, even if a tornado were to blow through enough junkyards to fill the whole Universe."[7] To put it more explicitly, chaos cannot generate order (we assume), even if there is no logical reason for it not to; yet if we look at biology, going back to the early works of Alexander Oparin in the 1920s, the primordial soup theory continues to be the only rational and reasonable explanation for the origin of life, as modified and enhanced by molecular genetics and the contemporary theory of evolution.[8] From that chaotic soup, we too were born, *pace* the principle of entropy, as Erwin Schrödinger explains: the fact that ordered physical structures, be it a galaxy or a sandcastle on the shore, tend to get spontaneously disordered, never the opposite.[9] Yet the conundrum, as problematic, murky, and mysterious as it seems, is not so much over the origin of life as it is over the origin of language (and consciousness, if they can be distinguished); but it is for this reason that no one has yet offered a coherent, stable, and shared theory that explains the path leading from a soup to sentences. We don't even know if one will ever be possible, at least in regard to language, or if it will remain a mystery to us forever.[10]

Before we move on to the next Lucretian argument, however, it is interesting to note that the order of the world, the recognizable one, the one that allows us to give names to things, is not necessarily tied to the stability of the observed object; on the contrary. Henri Atlan, who in a marvelous book published in 1979, *Entre le cristal et la fumée: Essai sur l'organisation de vivant* (Between smoke and crystal: An essay on the organization of the living), suggested these archetypes of crystal and smoke as the two models for everything. Thus, like smoke and crystal, water, words, sentences, and snowflakes become specific and natural examples of these general archetypes and, at first weakly and then with increasing strength, they raise challenging doubts as to the relationship between the world outside and the world within us. On the other hand, as Heraclitus warned, if we use an apparently simple term like *river* to indicate, for example, the specific stream of water that crosses Paris around the island on which the Notre-Dame stands, then we would have to change its name ten minutes later because the water in that spot would be different, whereas the river formerly located there would have already flowed downstream toward the sea. When it comes to understanding how we recognize things and give them names, things themselves seem to escape us, like the water of a river, and this suggests that chaos and order, the simple and the complex, are concepts much more mysterious than we first imagine. When it comes to words, objects look more like unseizable ghosts than concrete stones.

This dream of generating the complex from the simple is a constant across all sciences. But what is perhaps most surprising (though some might consider it to be least surprising) is that it was artists who were first to grasp it, at least in the contemporary era. The first such artist was, it seems to me, Paul Cézanne. If we can trust the words transcribed by one of his pupils, Émile Bernard, who met the painter when he was very old, the following intuition is pertinent:

> So, [Cézanne] explained to me all his ideas about shape, color, art, and the education of an artist: everything in nature is modeled on spheres, cones, and cylinders. One must learn to paint based on these simple figures, and only then can we do what we want.[11]

While we are unable to know the exact words uttered by Cézanne, this gloss is reasonably in line with what the Master wrote in his own hand in the letters to which we have access.

Let us pause here on the question of what creates order; a question that almost seems to have reintroduced the most radical of all cognitive oppositions: that between anomalists and analogists. This opposition originated in Greece during the Hellenistic period as a dispute over the criteria to be used in collecting texts for the most colossal human enterprise of all time: the collection housed by the library of Alexandria of Egypt of *every* text *ever* written.

On the one hand, the meaning of things—their "structure," as we would perhaps say nowadays—is seen as emerging from an unformed, infinite magma through the spontaneous development of symmetrical relations (analogy); on the other hand, structure would be formed by unforeseen and unforeseeable fractures in an immense lattice of symmetrical regularities, where everything would be otherwise inert, as it would be everywhere the same (anomaly). I have never been able to find anything more general than the contrast between anomalists and analogists: the entire world seems to me to be describable in one way or the other, *tertium non datur*. The point is that I can't decide whether to say "and" or "or": "one way *and* the other" or "one way *or* the other." Actually, the difficulty is only the result of a much deeper indecision: I can't tell whether analogy and anomaly are ways the world is organized or ways our way of seeing the world is organized. To tell the truth, I gave up on this problem some time ago: aside from not being able to solve it, I wouldn't even know whom to ask for an expert opinion. However, I do know that asking whether *the world* is organized according to analogy or anomaly is different from asking whether *language* is organized one way or the other. This distinction isn't hard to understand, because behind it is the idea that the structure of human language, that is to say the elements that make up language and the rules that combine these elements to form more complex structures, does not derive (or at least not completely) from the structure of the world. In brief, we could have an "anomalous" world and "analogous" language, or an "anomalous" language and an "analogous" world. All of this wouldn't be very relevant, or even very interesting, were it not for the fact that language wouldn't exist at all but for the activity of one thing (or really one thing for each person) in the world: the human brain.[12]

There is one more perspective I would like to mention. We have looked at those who, like Lucretius, believe that everything arises from chaos, and those who, like Cicero, think that chaos does not produce order but instead increases chaos. There is also an intermediate position, which essentially reproduces the hypothesis of the anomalists: that a "controlled" chaos—which is to say, the breaking of symmetries—could be the real engine of order in physics.[13] In terms of biology, the words of Alan Turing from his relatively little-known work dedicated to morphogenesis in biology come to mind: "It is suggested that a system . . . although it may originally be quite homogeneous, may later develop a pattern or structure due to an instability of the homogeneous equilibrium, which is triggered off by random disturbances. . . . The investigation is chiefly concerned with the onset of instability. It is found that there are six essentially different forms which this may take."[14]

Once again, we see that order and disorder are linked, and the link is based on a few, very few, types of ingredients, which are nevertheless capable of generating differences that appear qualitative to us. And once again these mechanisms, which we may regard as symmetry-breaking blind procedures applying to unstable structures, seem to drive a natural class of phenomena in human languages in the exact same way as in the physical world.[15] But here I really lack the imagination to express symmetry-breaking in language in a metaphorical way. We are in good company though, for Ferdinand de Saussure himself admitted that "we are on the contrary profoundly convinced that whoever treads on the territory of language, may be said to be abandoned by all the analogies of heaven and earth."[16] Nevertheless, before invoking Horace and the sky, we should once more listen to Lucretius.

3   TO DEVELOP

Lucretius explained to us how the world is broken up into tiny corpuscles and then he proposed a reason for their composition, but these explanations lead us to a new question: How can the forms and properties of things that exist start from an infinity of just a few kinds of corpuscles? Lucretius does not allow for magical interventions to explain the embryogenesis of things, and he states as much in a few very clear, rational, lapidary words:

> The growth of a body is a consequence of the original forms
> of the primitive elements that compose it.[1]

For Lucretius it is essential to note that no special interventions from the outside world will make things develop. The proof of this principle of compositionality crucially lies in reflecting on what can and cannot be original, that is, what is part of the inherent characteristics of the elements composing an object. This is a delicate and difficult problem. Witness the following claim, which sounds like an addendum for a reason:

> It should be added that in the totality of the universe not a single thing
> is born as a unique specimen and develops as such,

without belonging to a species with many of the same genus.[2]

The repetition of innumerable elements that belong to a species makes the idea of external interventions implausible or even impossible: An intervention would otherwise be needed for every object belonging to a species. Therefore, according to Lucretius, we would have a world of interventions as numerous as there are things that exist: Lucretius does not even comment on this, so ridiculous does he consider the hypothesis. The Gods, he explains to us repeatedly, don't exist, and thus they are not busy giving shape to each and every thing. Once the combination problem has been solved and the implausible notion of a world made up entirely of different things has been sidestepped, what remains may be the biggest problem of all. We see things (and not only objects) with certain properties and we understand that all these things come about through the combination of just a few types of primitive elements. The following question immediately emerges: How can we reduce these properties, which to us appear original and irreducible, to the few common things of which they are composed? Lucretius's approach to this question is that of a contemporary scientist: He chooses a minimum, controllable property, idealizing the world as if there were no other interfering phenomena, and focuses on it; that is, he implements the process that Edmund Husserl defines as the "Galilean method" (which applies not just to physics, as Noam Chomsky demonstrated when he adopted it to study human languages, and syntax in particular), and he does so by engaging in a thought experiment—or a *Gendankenexperiment*, as Albert Einstein called them. Lucretius concentrates on colors:

> Now listen to the words I have sought
> with difficulty and love so that you do not think that
> these white objects before your eyes are made up of white primitive elements;
> or that black objects are born of black seeds;
> nor any other thing imbued with any other color,
> do not believe they carry this and that color
> because their corpuscles of matter bear a similar color;
> for the corpuscles of matter have no color at all,
> be it the same or ultimately different.[3]

Lucretius is under no illusions; he does not stipulate that every property also belongs to primitive elements, "that these white objects before your eyes are made up of white primitive elements." He hypothesizes that some new properties emerge from elements that did not themselves possess them. Here lies one of the focal points to contemporary science (and philosophy): a profound understanding of the universe that becomes an explanation precisely because the explanation is less complex than what is observed. Perhaps a personal experience that has always amazed me since I was a kid, and one that many have undoubtedly shared, can help. When in the open sea, the blue of the water turns white if furrowed by the propellers of a boat: How is it possible that so much whiteness comes out of the blue sea, especially given that if we pick a small sample of that same water it turns out to be colorless? It was only years later I learned the explanation, but it's time now to put the matter aside and dive back into the sea that is made of words.

Lucretius's linguistic observation focuses on the letters of the alphabet that, when combined, form words, but we cannot escape the fact that even in language there are (other) emerging properties that are perhaps even more surprising. One is especially worth noting, and it is one that had already been explored and canonized by Aristotle. Let's take a word such as *girl*, add an article—*the girl*—and ask whether this is a sentence. The answer, evident to everyone from their first years of school but also on an intuitive basis, is that it is not. If we ask why, our intuition becomes a less reliable tool. Some will immediately state that a verb is missing, but if I add a verb to our two words and produce *the girl who runs*, the result still doesn't constitute a sentence. The most typical objection to it being one is that the verb *runs* in *the girl who runs* is part of the relative sentence *who runs* and a verb is rather needed in the main sentence; but this is an ungrounded objection from a logical point of view, because if one seeks a definition of "sentence," one cannot then exploit the notion of "sentence" to define it without getting caught in a circular, thus completely useless, procedure. Giorgio Graffi, in a fundamental essay on the history of syntax,[4] reminds us, citing, among others, John Ries,[5] that there have been more than a hundred and fifty different definitions of the notion of "sentence" since Aristotle, of which only nineteen are derived from texts written before the mid-1800s. The most famous and influential, and consciously non-comprehensive, of them remains the one Aristotle himself offered: A sentence is a sequence of words that allow one to determine whether they express a fact that is true or false. So, *the girl* isn't a sentence, nor is *the girl who runs*, but *the girl runs* fully qualify as one: It's true if the girl runs, and it's false if the girl doesn't run. Indeed, the minimal, ideal case of a sentence is the one with the verb *to be*, as in *the girl is the cause of the riot*. *The girl* is not a sentence—it is a noun phrase—nor is *the cause of the riot*—which is another noun phrase. They can both be subjects as in *the girl runs* or *the cause of the riot is obvious*. When they are combined with the verb *to be*, however, as in *the girl is the cause of the riot*, the former becomes a subject and the latter a predicate, denoting a property attributed to the subject, much in the same sense as *the girl causes the riot*. Many phenomena converge in illustrating that these two structures allowing permutation around the copula are not completely symmetric. For example, consider the two sentences *a picture of the wall was the cause of the riot* and *the cause of the riot was a picture of the wall*. Prima facie they look totally symmetrical, but they are not. Witness the following contrast: *which riot was a picture of the wall the cause of* versus *which wall was the cause of the riot a picture of*? The analysis and the impact of copular sentences would take us too far afield.[6] What matters here is that from two linguistic elements that do not have the property of conveying the true or the false in isolation a new linguistic element is generated when they are combined with the verb *to be*, yielding a sentence. As for the role of *to be*, as Aristotle already understood, we can take it to be simply an expression of tense when the word is not a verb. Witness pairs like *Mary caused the riot* versus *Mary was the cause of the riot*. The verb *to be* and its equivalent across languages, when it exists, is not a predicate: it is just the expression of tense. This link between *Mary* and *the cause of the riot* brings out a property—that very same property of being able to express truth or falsity, the core of sentencehood—which is not present in its parts in isolation. Metaphorically, it is like when two animals mate and give birth to a new animal that is neither the first nor the second: It is independent of both. This must be one of the reasons why in the Middle Ages the proposal to call the verb *to be* a "copula"—to convey the idea of the generation of the new by coupling subject and predicate—took root indelibly.[7] It must be noted, though, that Aristotle was aware of the fact that he hadn't solved all the problems pertaining to the definition of "sentence," and in fact he explicitly applied it only to a specific type of sentence—declarative sentences—and not to questions, prayers, or orders. And he didn't even apply it to all declarative sentences; for example, he was explicitly aware that his definition cannot apply to declarative sentences that refer to the future—such as *tomorrow there will be a naval battle*—because one cannot know whether they are true or false. In any case, Lucretius's thoughts encourage us to find similarities between the emergence of new properties in language and in the realm of things; the birth of sentences starting from words is certainly an emergent property within language, albeit a formal and nonphysical one.

Lucretius insists on this matter. Geniuses will sometimes demonstrate that they also participate emotionally in the thesis they are enunciating by using irony, as Dante did, for example, in another extraordinary and unfinished masterpiece of Western civilization, the *De vulgari eloquentia*, when he referred to the small village of Pietramala as the greatest city ever (we will be returning to this example). Lucretius does the same when he provides us with the surreal image of atoms that can laugh and talk:

> But if we think [. . .] that someone is capable of laughing
> who is not made of laughing atoms
> and who can reason with learned words and argue reasonably
> though not made of reasoning and speaking atoms,
> why can't we think that what we see as being sentient
> may not be formed of atoms devoid of sense perception?[8]

Lucretius's system is robust and consistent. The keystone to it is understanding that the properties *expressed* by the aggregates of corpuscles are not necessarily the properties *of* the corpuscles: They emerge from the combination of corpuscles.[9] Once more, Lucretius shows us how the world is structured by showing us how language is structured. But his discourse on language doesn't end there.

Lucretius makes a conceptual leap regarding language: from taking language as an analogical tool for explaining to seeing it as an object that itself needs an explanation. If we take this leap with him, we will start talking about the function of language rather than its structure. To do so we can refer to another classic author who often talked about language, Galileo Galilei; on the second day in the *Dialogue Concerning the Two Chief World Systems* he tells us:

> But above all stupendous inventions, what eminence of mind was that of the one who imagined he could find a way to communicate his deepest thoughts to any other person, even if distant by a very long interval of place and time? To speak with those who are in India, to speak to those not yet born nor will be for another thousand or ten thousand years? and how easily, with the various combinations of twenty characters on a page. [. . .] I have a booklet, much shorter than Aristotle and Ovid, in which all the sciences are contained, and with very little study others can form a very perfect idea of them: and this is the alphabet; and there is no doubt that the one who will be able to match and order this and that vowel well with those consonants or with those others, will obtain the most truthful answers to any question and will draw from them the teachings of all the sciences and all the arts.

This is something intuited by many, perhaps everyone, but it never ceases to amaze us. This human ability of breaking the world into parts, of associating words with properties and states and then reassembling them in accordance with new experiences, is truly unique to human beings. Animals may perhaps be able to associate words with things, and perhaps even with sensations and situations, but their dictionaries are a fixed repertoire of fixed sentences; ours are of words, and we can break up what we have recorded and put it back together to produce new and never-before-experienced meanings. This is why if I say *I saw a black swallow flying in the sky under a cloud with the shape of a whale*, nothing can prevent me from saying *I saw a whale with the shape of a cloud flying under a black swallow*. This is why we have fantasy and literature: because we have syntax. Animals do not.

We do not know if the world works as we describe it, or if the order of things follows a grammar in a more intimate sense than can be understood metaphorically, or if the properties we see are all that exists or if they are just a projection of what we are given to grasp—but by seeing it in terms of a combination of primitive elements, as Lucretius taught us, we at least begin to understand that *how* we describe the world tells us a lot about how we are made.

II

LANGUAGE AS AN OBJECT OF INQUIRY, OR THE QUESTION OF ORIGINS

Language was the tool Lucretius used to help us under-stand how the universe works; he used it as a model to make atomic theory credible. But now his attention shifts drastically: What does language *do*? The first three books of *De Rerum Natura* address the physical structure of the universe; after those, language goes from being an instru-ment for explanation to being an object of observation—observation that is no longer physical but psychological and biological and, in a certain sense, sociological. Of course, as with physics, Lucretius did not have access to the sophis-ticated knowledge that contemporary technology and sci-ence have made available to us today—that of genetics, evolution, and molecular genetics, for example—and it would certainly be futile to look for equivalents in his text. Nevertheless, Lucretius's reflection on language under this new perspective, even if reduced to pure speculation, can only give rise to admiration for the acumen with which he chooses his questions. As we continue our focus on his text we should note that compared to the first part, it will now present points that are not always as clear and coherent: I will not hide these contradictions nor emend them.

The first question, and the most general and obvious one, is what gave rise to language. Let us turn to Lucretius's answer:

> Then neighbors also began to join in friendship,
> in the desire not to hurt each other or suffer violence
> and they entrust children and women to each other,
> with some verbal stammering and gestures to express
> that everyone should have compassion for the weak.[1]

Here we immediately glimpse three of the constant features to explanations for the origins of language across cultures and times. *Place*: Language is born in a community of people who share a space—"neighbors," as Lucretius calls them. *Function*: Language is introduced to enable cooperation, be it to actively offer help to the weak or to passively reduce personal risk. *Development*: Language is born from stammers and gestures; it is not formed immediately and completely. These three characteristics remain unchanged in almost every subsequent explanation of language up to our contemporary ones; we will see reasons for and against them as we gradually prepare for our encounter with the fantastic beast, the bat with blue eyes.

One thing must be emphasized before we continue: Lucretius does not mention the diversity of languages, or rather, the fact that languages are not understandable to all people, which in itself is a major obstacle to this "cooperative" version of the birth of language. Lucretius does not mention the diversity of languages for the same reason that Western intellectuals would not mention it for centuries after: because the languages worthy of consideration were just politically affirmed languages, essentially Latin and ancient Greek. Greece's heritage, stemming from this poor opinion of other languages, manifests itself in the idea that those who spoke a foreign language seemed to stammer to the ignorant ear, leading the latter to consider it inferior. It is from this conviction of superiority that the Greek term for foreigners is "barbarian" (from the Ancient Greek "*oi bárbaroi*," literally "the stammerers")—a term so apt for its violence in that language that it retains this negative connotation today. Moreover, for those who instead became aware of other languages (I am obviously thinking of the Judeo-Christian tradition), Babel can only be seen as a punishment. It wouldn't be until medieval philosophy and more specifically Dante Alighieri's thought and research that the origin of this diversity would be seen in a new light, igniting the first general and rational reflections on many languages of the baroque era in the Port-Royal tradition and then maturing in the nineteenth century with comparative linguistics. Contemporary thinking on the matter, which has been often subject to both misunderstanding and ideological manipulation, has tried to understand if diversity really is a punishment or if instead, as I have tried to argue both in the form of an essay and a novel,[2] Babel is a gift, as are all differences, and the punishment is, if anything, indifference to this fact.

Of course, language is not the only thing that brings humans together and it is not necessary to look to the domain of ethics and culture to understand the need for cooperation. In fact, it would be enough to recognize a basic physiological necessity—the consequences of which on a social level are usually not even taken into consideration—to find another compelling reason: Every living being must sleep—we still do not completely understand why[3]—and therefore every living being needs to trust someone to defend them while they are helpless. "I sleep, therefore I trust someone," one could say. But let's not digress, and instead continue listening to Lucretius on the origin of language:

> Nature now forced the various sounds of language to be emitted
> and it was utility that established the names of things
> much as the incapacity to speak leads children to use gestures
> when they use their finger to show things that are present.
> Everyone senses the capabilities at their disposal and how to use them.[4]

Here Lucretius qualifies the force that has led to the condition of cooperation: He calls it a "utility" (*utilitas*, in Latin) that is, a tool suitable for use; a "natural tool" one might say. But the most important thing about this extraordinarily important passage is the observation that the instrumental function of language is not born with language; it precedes it. As evidence of this thesis, Lucretius cites the fact that children, to indicate things, do not wait to have the repertoire of available names: They indicate them with their fingers, that is, with gestures, and in doing so they realize that they are gifted of this force that, evidently, will then guide them from gestures to words.

5 HOW LANGUAGE IS BORN

To ask how language is born is to formulate a complex and two-pronged question. The first question involves distinguishing the different domains of observation: how language is born in a person (the ontogenetic domain) compared to how it is born in the human species (the phylogenetic domain). The second question is distinguishing the *function* of language from the *structure* of (a specific) language, which may only *seem* to be deeply connected. Lucretius not only knows how to reason and keep these themes separate;[1] he even demonstrates that he knows how to distinguish the level of linguistic ideation (or "verbalized thoughts") in the mind from that of the emission of words with the voice:

> So, when we express these voices from the depths
> of our body and emit them directly from the mouth,
> the moving tongue gives structure to the words, articulates
> and partially models them with the shape of the lips.[2]

These few words show us how profound his analysis of the phenomenon is: Lucretius clearly distinguishes the externalization of linguistic utterances, linked to the motor planning of the phonatory apparatus, from their "expression." The latter term, despite its etymology referring to the combination of the prefix *ex-* meaning "out" and *premere* meaning "to press," which could erroneously be interpreted as the act of squeezing the sound out of the body, does not refer to sound at all. In this passage, *express* rather refers to the process of choosing and composing words, which are rather squeezed from the mind, to form a sentence. It is a sophisticated distinction that even today not everyone adopts: We often speak tout court of "expression" without taking good account of inner, mental language, where words, even without the need to communicate anything to anyone, are thought with the sound associated with them, so-called inner speech or endophasic activity.[3] The act of uttering sounds is instead rendered with the verb *emit*, a compound of the same prefix *e-* (out) as in "express" but with the verb *mitto* meaning "to send." *Emit* means to "send out" of the mouth, as is explicitly clear from the words following it: *emit them directly from the mouth*. So, Lucretius distinguishes expression from emission to avoid misleading deductions.

In his explanation as to how language is born, Lucretius presents that incalculable intuition he implicitly hinted at with his reference to children's use of gestures. The next quote is important, beautiful, and in some ways, shocking:

Even before horns have sprouted on the calf's forehead,
when it becomes furious, it strikes us with its head bowed.
Panther cubs and lion cubs,
even when their teeth and claws have just erupted,
already defend themselves with nails, paws, and bites.

> And all species of birds rely on their wings and call on
> their feathers
>
> for help while still all flickering.[4]

For Lucretius, the attempt to satisfy a certain function precedes the birth of the organ that allows the expression of that function. Strictly speaking, this is only possible because the action is guided not by what is already available but by a force that precedes experience: instinct. It is therefore the instinct, not the organ itself, that guides development, both in us and in baby animals. By reversing the point of observation with respect to function, we understand that Lucretius is claiming that to perform a specific function we use what we will find in a future phase of development, but that function is already manifest before we even experience using the designated organ.

Lucretius has told us so far about animal functions such as fighting and flying; in the following verses, Lucretius reinforces this powerful and radical vision by referring instead to human beings, and combines the functions that today we would call motor functions, common to those he referred to for animals, with sensory functions:

> Make absolutely sure to escape from the vice of reasoning
> and prudently avoid that error of believing
> that the bright pupils of our eyes were created
> so that we become able to see and that the upper parts
> of our legs and thighs which rest on the feet can bend
> to enable us to take long strides,

or that our arms have been attached to strong forearms
and that either side has been given hands as tools
so that we might do what we need to in life.[5]

Lucretius's recommendation is clear: He invites us to remember that our eyes do not grow to satisfy the function of seeing; on the contrary, we see because our eyes have grown.

Lucretius's text is not always free from interpretative difficulties, sometimes due to contradictions, but we can say with reasonable certainty that the distinction between two independent forces acting in the organization of the biological world is clear: there is instinct (which precedes the organ and may well not be expressed) and organ development. Those who confuse the two, assuming organs grow to satisfy the instinct, are simply wrong. It would take Charles Darwin to establish a global vision of biological development and lead us to reflect on the progressive, blind, and random changes that evolution beings about and on the selective capacities of organs and functions, but Lucretius has already identified the cardinal points of biological observation: in particular, those that dissolve the teleological and—one could say—magical interpretations of nature. Lucretius told us about these two forces in animals and humans with respect to relatively trivial and common functions with animal organisms: vision and locomotion. Strengthened by these premises, he can now present the culmination of his reasoning and connect this powerful and new vision about sight and movement to sound and language specifically:

Any other function that is interpreted in this way

is interpreted backward and contrary to logic,

since nothing is born of the body so we can make use of it;

on the contrary, what is born generates use.

Sight was not born before pupils

nor the sound of words before the tongue.

On the contrary, tongue long preceded the capacity to make a discourse with words

and ears were created long before sound was heard:

in short, I think, all organs existed before their use.

They could not develop through use.[6]

I'll rewrite a sentence from this quotation for emphasis: "tongue long preceded the capacity to make a discourse with words." Lucretius is using the Latin word *lingua*, here translated as "tongue": in both languages, Latin and English, this word is ambiguous. It can mean either the organ in the mouth or (a specific) language. In the context of saying that the tongue preceded the capacity to make discourse with words, the appropriate meaning of *tongue* must be the organ, if we want this thought to be consistent with the one regarding the eyes and ears. In other words, as we would say today by reversing the famous motto attributed to Jean-Baptist Lamarck:[7] It is *not* function that makes organs develop. This interpretation of *tongue* as an organ is also indirectly reinforced by the other terms Lucretius uses in this quotation: He clearly distinguishes the capacity to construe a discourse (*orare*) with words (*dictis*) as being different from the tongue—in short, he distinguishes grammar from speech. All in all, by assembling segments of Lucretius's text, we are coming to terms with a complex view: on the one hand, there is grammar, the capacity to construe a discourse with words, and that depends on the natural instinct to obtain the utility that accompanies the emergence of cooperation between individuals; on the other hand, there is an organ, the tongue, that was created before its use to produce sounds to make words and sentences. The instinct meets the organ and they constitute human language. Confusing or conflating these two concepts and the order in which they appear would amount to misinterpreting the core thought of Lucretius.

Finally, to reinforce his vision, Lucretius even makes an argument that today we would define as "clinical," though objectively incorrect, according to our modern understanding of the nonstandard conditions humans often face:

> It is not easy to persuade the deaf through reason what must be done;
>
> they would not tolerate, nor long endure, the sounds of voices
>
> they have never heard repeated rumbling in their ears without any effect.[8]

The interesting fact here is that Lucretius, who has just distinguished organ from function, nevertheless powerfully binds language—at least with respect to the physical capacity of the emission of linguistic expressions—to the organism: He understands that, at least in the sense of communication, biological limitation is not surmountable by the force of reason. No exercise can restore the ability to hear sounds in a deaf person, just as no exercise can regrow an amputated hand. Lucretius is expressing once more, albeit through different arguments, the same idea that function does not make the organ: He tells us that not only a merely optional function but even a real necessity can change nature.

This is not surprising: How useful it would be for the human species, always subjected to the need to be hydrated, to grow the ability to drink seawater. The history of our species, strictly linked throughout evolution to our environmental resources, would change radically if this were possible: Many populations could live in desert areas that are close to the sea. But such a choice is just not possible because we are limited by our biological structure. And note also that Lucretius never speaks of language-learning as explicit teaching; he speaks only and always of an instinct: This is the underlying and compelling driving force for humans. In the years during which Lucretius is writing, the idea of instinctive learning was not new. A contemporary of Lucretius, Marco Terentius Varro, in *De lingua latina* (X 15) wrote: "I call *nature* the case in which we all do not ask how to decline a name but we decline it ourselves." Crucially, note that Varro doesn't refer to how we *infer* the meaning or the existence of a certain noun from the observation of the world, but rather to how we *decline* a given name, whatever it is; that is, how we construct the system or, technically, the paradigm of the forms that constitute the declension of that noun according to number, gender, case, person, and all the other features a language may or may not display. And similarly for all the other parts of speech. This capacity is so strong that even if I give you a sentence of invented words, such as for example *the gulk ganfles the brals* which we encountered before, you may not be able to judge if it is true or false; but if I ask you what happened to the brals you can immediately tell with no instructions whatsoever that the brals have been ganfled by the gulk, as predicted by Varro in the case of unknown names.[9]

This sensitivity, this reasoning immerses the discussion of language development in the great theme of development in general. We noted how Lucretius explained to us that the shapes of primitive elements are not infinite. Here the discussion moves on to the possible forms of compounds of primitive elements. These too are not infinite precisely because they develop as a consequence of the specific and limited properties of the primitive elements that compose them.

Language is not exempt from this powerful vision even if here the minimal elements are not corpuscles but other types of primitives, such as those which are associated in signs to generate sounds and meanings. Lucretius could not have known that even for language there exist possible and impossible languages, starting from new primitive elements first discovered in the twentieth century: first in phonology, then in syntax, morphology, and semantics.[10] The first step was taken on a formal and comparative basis: In the 1950s, Noam Chomsky, along with other scholars such as Joseph Greenberg and later Richard Kayne (see references to these authors in the bibliography), heirs of Saussure's structuralism in different ways, understood that grammar is a selective system and that not all conceivable rules are realized in the languages of the world.[11] The second step was to link these limitations to the neurobiological structure of the human brain, dispelling the fear of Eric Lenneberg who, in a fundamental book on the biological foundations of language, which included a foundational essay by Chomsky, wrote: "A biological research on language must seem the more paradoxical as it is so widely assumed that languages consist of arbitrary, cultural, conventions."[12] To summarize: Today we know that the structure of the universe that emerges from *De Rerum Natura*, deriving the existence of possible and impossible forms as an expression of the primitive elements that compose them, is equally true for human languages, although the primitive elements in question are different. It cannot escape our attention that Lenneberg's and Chomsky's innovative seminal books were published in the 1960s, whereas *De Rerum Natura* by Cicero shortly after 54 BCE: twenty centuries stand between two astonishingly converging views.

To understand these two steps in the revolution of contemporary linguistics, it is useful to start from the formal one and concentrate on one simple case of an impossible rule or, better, a single class of impossible rules. For example, there are no rules based on the linear order of words in a linguistic expression in any language of the world. Everything is explained only in terms of hierarchical "groupings" between words in "phrases" or "constituents." A simple example suffices. Let's take as a noun a proper name like *Mary*, constituting a noun phrase made of a single word. Noun phrases can be made of more than one word: for example, you can have *books*, *books about her*, *the books about her*, *the nice books about her*, *the nice books*, and so on, expanding the noun *book* with other elements gravitating—so to speak—around a noun, potentially without any upper limit but those imposed by memory and physiological limits of human body. In these examples, *books* is called "the head" of the noun phrase. Technically, it is said that a noun phrase can be nested or boxed within another noun phrase. Consider a noun phrase like *those friends of Mary*. Now let's take a simple rule such as the agreement of the subject with the verbal predicate: If I just take *Mary* and the verb *to run* I will have *Mary runs*. But if instead of *Mary* I take a larger noun phrase like *those friends of Mary* and combine it with the verb *to run*, I will get *those friends of Mary run* and not *those friends of Mary runs*. Grammar has rendered *Mary*, so to speak, "invisible" to the verb. Even if this proper name *Mary* precedes the verb *run* in the linear sequence of words exactly as in the previous case, the verb sees only the head of the larger noun phrase (in this case, *friends*) and agrees with it. This simple example extends to all the rules of every language in the world, whether or not they involve agreement. It's a fact that grammars do not see linear order but phrases within the (potentially infinite) hierarchical two-dimensional organization of words. To put it simply, there are no "flat rules" in any language of the world. This is quite surprising even from a general cognitive view. The only uncontroversial property of language, *qua* physical, namely the fact that words are arranged in a sequence, doesn't count: It is ignored by the speaker both as an adult or a child. Reality matters, but the way we see it matters even more. Perhaps all theories, insofar as they have an explanatory force, are modeled on grammars as filters.

The second revolutionary step forward, the neurobiological one, is instead based on a series of experiments that I am going to illustrate synthetically. A group of healthy monolingual subjects were asked to learn possible rules and impossible rules based on linear order in a foreign language and were then asked to judge if sentences construed with those rules were grammatical or not. Using methods based on neuroimaging, it was clearly seen that the human brain recognizes impossible rules with no explicit instruction or indication and computes those rules through neuronal networks that are different from those canonically involved in natural languages. More specifically, the core result was that Broca's area activity, one of the crucial points of the natural network for language,[13] (a) progressively augmented—as expected—when the subjects' accuracy in judging the grammaticality of the sentences following possible rules augmented, whereas (b) it was progressively and partially inhibited when the subjects' accuracy in judging the grammaticality of the sentences following impossible rules augmented. This is what is technically called "a double dissociation"—the ideal experimental result when two dependent variables are measured. This provided robust evidence that the rules of human languages do not consist of "arbitrary cultural conventions" (referring to Lenneberg's influential caveat) but are the expression of the brain's neurobiological structure that precedes any experience. This is in a sense tautological since, of course, we cannot conventionally decide which particular part of the brain to use. Interestingly, two separate but strongly related experiments based on this common paradigm were carried out with two distinct teams (besides myself) in two labs with different statistical methods: The only points in common were the use of an fMRI, and two sets of possible versus impossible rules. But the major distinction was that one experiment utilized two real languages belonging to two different language families (Italian and Japanese, while the subjects were monolingual German native speakers); the other utilized invented words, technically "pseudo words," as in Lewis Carroll's famous "Jabberwoky." As with the example used before, *The gulk ganfles the brals*, this was done to avoid the subject inferring the syntactic structure from the word's meaning. Moreover, the number of errors the subjects made by the end of training was compared to the errors they made in their own language, proving that the difference was not based on complexity but depended on whether the rules were possible or impossible, that is, hierarchically organized or instead based on linear order (flat rules).[14] This distinction must precede any experience: It is built into our organisms on a genetic basis. I prefer not to use the term "innate" as I would not use it for any biologically determined trait: Nobody would say that we have an "innate face," but the biological instructions for our faces to grow are surely part of our genetic endowment. In fact, beyond minimal differences in the extremely complex system of genetics, we all have the same face.

Lucretius, right at the beginning of his poem, had already seen very clearly that the limits of the world were inscribed in the development of things before any experience. He tells us so in a concise and elegant way, and now we can quote him in a new context:

> from this [Epicurus], victorious, tells us what is possible and what is impossible,
>
> and finally, the reason for each thing's limited potential and deeply inherent boundary.[15]

Lucretius did know that for a theory to have explanatory value, what counts is not what it catalogs but what it excludes; in the case of language, it is a matter not of collecting together and comparing known languages but of developing a theory of impossible languages. Collecting and comparing languages becomes really revealing once the theory of impossible languages has clarified the limits at which language changes—when history and all other possible factors intervene.[16] Of course, the development of languages throughout the centuries can also be indirectly exploited to test the theory of impossible languages, as in the seminal works by Longobardi et al.[17] More generally, this issue is infinitely important if we are to increase our understanding of the zeitgeist of any culture within the boundaries of Babel such as in the works of Mancini and Tomasin.[18]

Lucretius, then, returns to animals, preceding in a sense the same kind of reasoning Descartes would employ many centuries later in his *Discourse on Method*. He had just presented the example of hornless lambs and toothless panthers and lion cubs to convince us of our own uniqueness:

So, if the different senses force animals,

although speechless, to emit different voices,

how much more just and natural that men back then

could have given names to different things with different sounds![19]

Humanity is a singularity: Lucretius doesn't say this explicitly; perhaps he doesn't feel it is compatible with the atomic view of the world. Nevertheless, his words implicitly recognize this fact. In fact, that humanity is a singularity was recognized in other cultures that preceded Lucretius: the Jewish tradition as expressed in the Torah, for example. To the best of my knowledge, Genesis is the only known case of a God who sits down and listens to his creatures: "Whatever man called each of the living beings, that must have been his name" (Gen. II, 19:1); of course, God lets them create names, not things, but perhaps it is precisely because of this act of freedom that humans can be considered similar to God. What could be a paradigmatic case of the singularity of humanity if not this? In any case, this uniqueness would not be properly recognized by modern scientists until Descartes who, through the framework of scholastic thought, recognized it in an explicit and rational (which is to say, not theological) way. Lucretius simply starts from this singularity to say that if it were not so, then it would be unfair and unnatural (*aequum* is Lucretius's word) if humans did not speak but animals instead could express themselves in verses.

Once the interplay between necessity and instinct and the specificity of human beings has been clarified, it still remains to be understood how language was born from this community of beings. Here Lucretius draws on all his rationality to answer. Obviously, he cannot turn to genetics (let alone Mendelian normolecular genetics)[20] and can only draw on reason. The result is astonishing, and the reasoning is flawless, given the premises:

> Therefore, to believe there was a time when one man assigned names
> to things and that from this fact other men learned their first words
> is delusional. Indeed, why would he have been able to name everything
> with words and utter the various sounds of the tongue
> and others could not have done the same thing?[21]

If language is born of the need for cooperation and nature makes it available to us as an instinct, it cannot be born from a single person because all people have the need for cooperation and, all being endowed with the same nature, it must be an instinct common to everyone. Language, for Lucretius, does not have a single origin and cannot be a singularity among humans: It is born wherever there are people. This also eliminates the misleading and incoherent notion that language is an invention, because inventions, genuine inventions, are typically born from a single person, some from several people but certainly not from everyone.

Lucretius is well aware that he has anchored language to nature, to the organism of humans, and to their biological structure, and he reinforces this position by reiterating it in the context of the question of how language originated:

> Moreover, if others also did not exchange words,
> how could the notion of their usefulness have taken root
> in anyone? And where did someone first get the ability
> to know and see in the mind what one wants to do?
> Likewise, one alone could not coerce multiple people
> to learn the names of things against their will.[22]

This is the logical consequence of what he had said about those born deaf and in general about the relationship between organs and functions: If only one person had the instinct for language or the ability to use it, then that person would have remained silent because language would have had no effect on those who did not share the same ability. Therefore, by logical necessity, given the rational tools he possessed, Lucretius's conclusion could only be that language must have been born simultaneously in many people and only then could language be used for the purposes of cooperation and utility he was referring to.

Lucretius thus concludes his tapestry on the structure and birth of language, the ideal counterpart to that other tapestry he presented in which language was not the object of the tapestry but the means to understanding it. We could stop here but, as we said, we believe in the power of the classics to help us formulate new questions and perhaps allow us to adopt new perspectives even if by contradicting them.

There is a conceivable challenge to Lucretius's observation. It comes from a modern philosopher who formulated a hypothesis about an impossible type of language that leads us to consider the degree to which communication is connected to language—the way ears are to sound. The philosopher is Ludwig Wittgenstein, who in his *Philosophical Investigations* (I: 344) asks: "Is it conceivable that people never speak an audible language, but should nevertheless talk to themselves inwardly, in the imagination?" It is a question that cannot be answered, because it's not a real question: It's a provocation that stimulates us into thinking of a possible world in which we all have a language, but one that we don't use with others—a world in which everyone speaks their own private language. This notion of a silent people is not original to Wittgenstein and evokes an eighteenth-century text by Giambattista Vico in which he gives a name to this phase of humanity's development and calls humans "Mutes" (*Mutoli* in Italian, which sounds in this language like the name of a population):

> Mutes make themselves understood by gestures or objects that have natural relationships with the ideas they want to signify. This axiom is the principle of the hieroglyphs by which all nations spoke in the time of their first barbarism. It is also the principle of the natural speech which Plato (in the *Cratylus*) and after him Iamblichus (*On the Mysteries of the Egyptians*) guessed

to have been spoken in the world at one time. Their view was shared by the Stoics and by Origen (*Against Celsus*); but, since it was but a guess, it was opposed by Aristotle (in his *On Interpretation*), and by Galen (in his *Doctrines of Hippocratis and Plato*). The dispute is discussed by Publius Nigidius in Aulus Gellius. This natural speech must have been succeeded by the poetic discourse of images, similes, comparisons and natural properties.

Languages must have begun with monosyllables, for [even] in the present abundance of articulated [i.e., polysyllabic] words into which children are now born they begin with monosyllables in spite of the fact that in them the fibers of the organ necessary to articulate speech are very flexible.[23]

The key phrase in this passage is, without any doubt, "natural relationships with ideas." With this, Vico introduces a sort of "conceptual onomatopoeia," that is, a natural correlation between ideas and gestures, a relationship similar to that of the few words in languages that imitate the real sounds of animals or objects associated with them (e.g., *meow* or *roar*).

But in the history of humanity, there is no evidence of the existence of Vico's "Mutes," just as we have no evidence of Wittgenstein's exclusively silent concepts and private mental languages. This is even more interesting since we all experience inner speech. What is to be excluded is a civilization made up of only inner speakers. On the other hand, as illustrated a few pages earlier, there is robust evidence that certain languages are impossible in the sense defined there, as a consequence of the neurobiological architecture of our brain. These biological boundaries of Babel establish the space within which cultural trends, politics, chance, and individual inventions of a given point in time can shape grammars.[24] With this notion of impossible languages, we will show in the next chapter how Lucretius's questions on the origin of language can be answered today.

6 THE BAT WITH BLUE EYES

Lucretius's explanation of the birth of language is very clear: Language is the tool with which a natural need for cooperation, imprinted in all individuals as an instinct by nature, manifests itself and expresses itself by exploiting, in the mature phase of the individual's development, the organ of the tongue; it was born progressively, starting from simple forms still visible today in animals. It's all "explained," we would say if we were to speak etymologically. And yet, the classics have, among other special powers, that of encouraging us to question everything. *De Rerum Natura* allows us to better understand how things can be explained, as well as to see them with new eyes and new tools. To do so, I would like to discuss a special creature, an imaginary fantastic beast: a bat with blue eyes.

Everyone knows many people with blue eyes even if they are in the minority: They constitute about one-tenth of the world's population. How do blue eyes come to be? They follow genetic instructions, something we had already known even before the molecular structure of genes was deciphered, and which was evident from the statistical distribution of this characteristic in the descendants of pairs of parents according to the Mendelian model. We also know that, leaving aside the difference in their frequency, blue eyes occur in many parts of the world. This is not surprising given that they depend on genetic instructions common to all individuals of our species.

Moving on to bats: They have been populating the night skies for 50 million years, long before we came onto the scene. They are mammals, similar in appearance to rodents, but they fly like birds; their taxonomical order is called *chiroptera*, which literally means "with hands that act like wings" (*cheir* meaning "hands" and *pterux* "wings," in ancient Greek). The surprising fact is that bats appeared suddenly in the world, in the sense that between them and their nonflying ancestors, rats, there were no "intermediate" animals—so to speak—that exhibited forms of transition between the limbs of those that don't fly and those that do. In other words, there existed no such things as semi-bats.

Which brings us to our imaginary creature, the bat with blue eyes. This is nothing more than an opportunity to rethink the origin of language in a radical way, without, however, abandoning the idea that language develops instinctively through our biology, rather than by instruction or imitation. In a paper published in the journal of the American National Academy of Sciences (*PNAS*), Karen Sears and her research team found an answer to the absence of intermediate animals between bats and their flightless ancestors, showing once more that absences can be very powerful engines in research development. Bat embryos initially have bones similar to those of their nonflying relatives, but at a certain point in development the bones of the hands grow dramatically and connect to the patagium, the vascularized membrane that supports them in flight. This happens as a result of the expression of a single protein that regulates bone growth, which is controlled by a single specific gene, BMP2 (the acronym comes from *bone morphogenetic protein*).[1] This binary behavior explains the absence of intermediate animals. Everything is regulated by a single gene that makes the difference. It's like a switch: If it is activated, wings appear; if it is not activated, paws remain.

Before commenting further, let's consider the other physical trait of our fantastic beast: its blue eyes. In another work, published this time in another American journal, *Science*, Hans Eiberg and his research group have shown, by comparing the regions of the genome that contain the coding for the color of blue eyes in 800 people expressing this trait, from all parts of the world, that in all probability it is a single mutation that impacted a single person who lived about 10,000 years ago in the Black Sea region, one that takes place in a single gene, the OCA2 (here the acronym comes from *oculocutaneous albinism* gene, i.e., the skin and eye albinism gene). Eiberg also observed that the spread of this trait in northern Europe and Russia may have produced, through a Darwinian selective basis, both functional advantages and greater mating attractiveness.[2] Whatever may have happened, blue eyes weren't born here and there in the populations of the world; that is, this characteristic is not like a surname that, for various reasons, could arise and spread regionally through different countries, for example as a consequence of trade routes, such as *Smith* or *Brown* or their Italian equivalents *Ferrari* or *Moro*, corresponding to crafts or physical traits. Blue eyes arose from a single person due to the random mutation of a single gene in a single location, not scattered in different parts of the world. Their appearance is similar to that of red poppy flowers in a field: They depend on the seed of a single flower that turned red in a past mutationt; they do not turn red through their own initiative.

Reality surprises us the more counterintuitive it is: Our imaginary beast, the bat with blue eyes, flew in from the realm of metaphor and took on the shape and meaning of concrete fact, providing us with the plausible biological and independent information we need in order to shed light on the question of the origin of language. Let us now combine the two biological facts, pertaining to wings and eyes, and return to language. On the one hand, the fact that all people with blue eyes, male or female, have only one common unique ancestor with blue eyes allows us to maintain the hypothesis that language, which is also the result of genetic instructions and not cultural invention, was born in a precise point of the world and not in a widespread way—not in a patchy manner, so to speak. On the other hand, the development of wings in bats fulfills a need, while at the same time it demonstrates that certain organs take shape discontinuously—which is to say, in a sudden manner, as modern biologists recognized.[3] This also immediately reminds us of Lucretius's words: It is not need that makes an organ grow. Mice, after all, would benefit from the ability to fly; it would aid them in accessing food sources and would help them escape from prey, but biological development is not about recognizing a need and influencing the will. Mice don't fly because the gene that controls hand-bone development isn't activated in them the way it is in bats. Similarly, we can't drink sea water even if millions of people living close to the ocean are thirsty.

In the same way, all animals have a need to communicate, and arguably plants do as well,[4] but only humans have received not only the instinct but also a structural mutation that allows grammars to flourish in our brains within certain boundaries: tools that by recombining a few discrete elements allow us to build ever new and potentially infinite messages, whether by way of sounds (or signs) for words or words for sentences. That said, nature has also imposed constraints on us—the boundaries of Babel—outside which there can only exist impossible languages. Here, too, that same passage from Lucretius resonates, when he tells us that Epicurus explained "what is possible and what is impossible, and finally, the reason for each thing's limited potential and deeply inherent boundary."

This limit, which at first sight seems like an obstacle, is actually a fortunate event (in fact, a necessary one) because children all over the world save time in the process of acquiring language, as they avoid having to calculate the relationships between all words in a sentence that would obey impossible grammars, such as all those based on linear order (remember how grammar was able to make "Mary" invisible in a noun phrase in the previous chapter). The boundaries of Babel, in other words, are a sort of natural sieve that reduces the time needed for spontaneous acquisition within the limits allowed by nature. Otherwise, if every combination of words had to be checked, from a purely combinatorial view, it would take much longer than it does to compute a sentence with a few words. A sieve that precedes experience is biologically determined, and it must be compatible with all existing grammars (as well as those that will exist, have existed, and may never exist); a sieve, that is, which in a sense captures what I like to call the "stem mind" of all children in terms of their linguistic abilities: a mind capable of expressing any language, just as a stem cell can specialize as any type of cell. The process of selection among a superabundant repertoire of grammars constituting the stem mind has been associated with a complex process known as "neural network pruning," the reduction of the synapses' contacts, which have their peak on average around ninth months after birth. This process, on average, takes about five years after birth.[5] Notably, the first person who developed the idea of learning by selection was Niels Jerne, a biologist who likened some core aspects of the formation of the immune system to the spontaneous acquisition of human languages by children. His Nobel lecture, "The Generative Grammar for the Immune System," highlights the force of the linguistic model.[6] His revolutionary thought was to assume that each of us is born with a superabundant repertoire of antibodies for diseases that we may never encounter. Needless to say, the first person he cites in his Nobel lecture is Noam Chomsky.

The gift of Babel is thus manifest. The fact that individuals of the human species do not all understand each other has perhaps played a fundamental, positive role in keeping communities contained, or in any case of such a size as to be able to manage the concrete needs of daily life and thus also limit epidemics. This sort of containment also plays a role with other animals and possibly in the microbiological domain, but it occurs through the reductive power of diseases (an intuition that goes back at least to Volterra and references cited there).[7] Had all humans understood each other, it would actually have been very difficult not to avoid extinction. Therefore, the logical conclusion is unexpected and contrary to tradition: Not only is Babel not a punishment for humanity, but it turns out to have been a gift.[8] Whether or not it is still a gift is a challenging question in a global world where technology seems to change the rules of the game for humans. In any case, so far, Babel has been a gift.

But regardless of the advantages and disadvantages of the boundaries of Babel, the fact is that human beings have limits. Sometimes the limits are useful and rational (as in the way we perceive the passage of time in an organized fashion, with a past, a present, and a future); other times, they seem to be completely unmotivated and useless, if not counterproductive (as when we instinctively believe that of two objects with the same shape but different weight, the heavier one will reach the ground first when they are dropped).[9] In any case, knowing these limits is a necessary step to understanding who we are, and Lucretius, who emphasizes the value of the intrinsic limits programmed into things and organisms, sheds the brightest light on this issue.

On the other hand, the fact that there are no intermediate animals with intermediate wing shapes, that is, no stages between bats and their flightless relatives, strongly suggests another powerful analogy with language: It makes it biologically plausible that some core aspects of language could have arisen en bloc, without the existence of intermediate grammatical structures between ours and that of all other animals. Obviously, the first individual who had this mutation and those who inherited it (the Bible actually says that it was a woman, Eve, who spoke first—although this fact couldn't be accepted by many males, including Dante who in *De vulgari eloquentia* dared correct the sacred text) couldn't use it for many generations: There was of course no vocabulary at first, only a potentiality. It was just the first stem mind, from a linguistic point of view. It must have been like the inventor of the telephone who, holding the first receiver in his hand, wondered whom he could call. Therefore, even if language was born en bloc and the sudden result of a single mutation, we must still imagine that it went through phases of progressive evolution over time; this is surely the case with the lexicon, that is, the set of words of our dictionary, especially nouns, adjectives, and verbs. It can't have grown instantly; it must have taken decades or centuries to form a stable, potentially infinite lexicon, describing qualities, objects, and relations and a finite set of words, like articles, preposition, or the copula, to link the other ones together. After all, even in our single individual life we see the birth of new words. But when it comes to syntax, it's a different story: Since syntax in a nutshell is the ability to assemble discrete objects such as words into sentences, and since obviously there is no upper limit to the potential length of a sentence (just as in arithmetic there is no great-est number), we must *necessarily* admit that syntax did arrive en bloc, unless we accept the idea that the infinite can arrive piecemeal—say, first a quarter, then a half, and then a whole. This would amount to stating that humanity first counted up to, say, seventeen, then to twenty-two, and then on to infinity: Infinity either exists all at once or it doesn't exist. This is a logical fact, not an empirical hypothesis—and one that was already well-known to Aristotle as being a distinction between potentiality and actuality.

Language, therefore, or at least the syntactic nucleus of all human languages, is born in one piece, like arithme-tic, and is used to satisfy the needs of human cooperation, but it is not an invention, just as ears and eyes aren't. As Lucretius said, it is an instinct that is expressed after an organ develops independently. This instinct took the form of grammar only after a genetic mutation occurred in a single individual, who then transmitted it to their offspring. Ever since then, this mutation has allowed the organ called language to "grow" and interface with the parts of our body that are sensitive to aspects of communication such as speaking and hearing (anatomically, the articulatory appa-ratus and the ears, but not exclusively so if one considers facial expressions, for example, or sign language), devel-oping the lexicon in the way just mentioned. Otherwise, humans would have remained like children and primates, pointing with our fingers and making a few other signs, without the infinite power of syntactically combining dis-crete elements. This vision is completely counterintuitive, of course: It is easier to imagine that the need to speak arose in all human beings and was then channeled into the mouth to give birth to words and grammar together with the passage of time. Yet, in a similarly naive, albeit understandable, first interpretation, the wings of bats also seem like the perfect and final result of a series of progressive attempts to generate tools for flying and allow us to imagine imprecise, unsuitable and, what matters more, nonexistent prototypes. We now have evidence that a family of mice did not gradually turn into bats: The transformation manifested itself suddenly and, as with blue eyes, in a single individual, male or female, who carried this specific mutation (whether ultimately it be regarded as a positive or negative mutation, we cannot yet say). So even the hypothesis of syntax being born suddenly en bloc, initially flanked by an "embryo dictionary" that has by necessity grown progressively, is now even biologically plausible, supporting the deductions elaborated on comparative and deductive grounds. It's certainly a counterintuitive hypothesis, but it's not unusual for science to countenance these kinds of thoughts: From the movement of the Sun with respect to the Earth to the fall of bodies of different weights, nature presents us with immediate intuitions that may turn out to be wrong but that reason nevertheless allows us to correct. Apparently, having limits on our understanding of reality, even with a false interpretation as in the case of the rate at which objects fall with different weights, is better than having no limits at all, which can paralyze us with too much information.

The bat with blue eyes presents a new way of continuing along the path charted out by Lucretius; but it also, of course, has generated new questions, questions probably more numerous than answers. But having more questions than answers is a good sign that we have a productive way of exploring reality and formulating hypotheses. These questions sprang and blossomed from the impetuous pages of *De Rerum Natura* and confirm how ahead of his time Lucretius was when he imagined that language was a natural instinct that preceded the birth of the tongue and was not an invention.

Our journey into the theme of language as conceived by Lucretius in *De Rerum Natura* ends here. A partial, subjective journey, indeed, and one full of omissions for many, with some perhaps overly personal asides, but such is the inevitable impact of the classics. They represent each and every person's special heritage and as such they encourage each of us to pursue different paths. My hope is therefore not to convince anyone of anything but to share ideas that struck me in reading this classic in the hope that this personal reading will encourage others to derive the same joy.

If I had to use a single sentence to summarize what Lucretius has transmitted to me, I would say that it is the confirmation of a radical reversal of a traditional vision: When it comes to humans, it is the flesh that has become *logos*—the Word.

III

THE ALPHABET AND THE PLAGUE: WHAT REMAINS OF REASON

What is there to say after reading a reading of Lucretius? It depends on the reader, of course, but I myself have two remaining unexpected and independent points to share: one explicit and one implicit. Let's start with the easier of the two.

7 THE ORDER OF THOUGHTS: DESCARTES AND THE DREAM OF A PERFECT LANGUAGE

Lucretius, using the model of the alphabet, convinces us that the atomic hypothesis of the universe—the nature of things—is plausible. There are not an infinite number of types of different things. Everything we observe is the result of infinite copies of a few types of elements that, due to their specific shape, are driven by random movement to aggregate and express new properties that the shapes themselves did not originally possess. However, this credible and fascinating hypothesis leaves us with a new problem, which Lucretius does not invoke but which is logically valid: Is there any order among the basic elements themselves? Can this order manifest itself in the aggregates they form? We are led to formulate these questions by Lucretius's metaphorical use of language, specifically by the primitive elements of this language: the letters of the alphabet. Indeed, in Western alphabets, as everyone knows, letters have a rigid order, an order that comes from a distant history in time and space, which starts from Mesopotamia and Egypt and was perhaps originally born in order to provide organization to archives for commercial, social, and religious functions. Whatever the history of the alphabet—indeed, of alphabets—may in fact be,[1] the problem of the order of the primitive elements is clear: In the case of the alphabet, it is certainly no coincidence that the meaning of the word *alphabet* alludes precisely and solely to the *relative* order of the first two letters (*alpha* and *beta*): There appears to be no reason for any letter to precede any other in the alphabet. This same problem of the rationale for a basic order arises whenever we speak of any primitive elements.

In fact, the problem of the order of primitive elements, even if Lucretius does not deal with it directly, cannot fail to arise when reading his text; it certainly arose for me, as it has for many others. It is enough just to recall those central and revolutionary words of his about the power of letters: *even when their order alone is permuted*. Here something happens that can only happen with the classics: A classic evokes other classics. Reading Lucretius and his insistence on the question of order reminded me of the words of another giant and something he expressed in a relatively neglected text. I'm speaking of Descartes and his letter to Father Mersenne, a renowned philosopher and mathematician. In this letter, a relatively neglected manuscript, dated November 20, 1629, Descartes replied to his longtime friend Father Mersenne, who had asked him for an opinion about the project of a mutual friend—probably the mathematician and polyglot Claude Hardy. The project, which is not mentioned in any other source, consisted in the proposal of the construction of an artificial language that could be learned "in five or six hours." Descartes, without hesitation, completely and irrevocably demolishes this proposal with a series of exemplary reasons, ranging from the difficulty of constructing valid sounds for all languages to the fact that an invented language without literature, if not an epic, is practically useless (those who know J. R. R. Tolkien's invented languages know this well); his reaction, however, goes far beyond the *pars destruens* and he offers an alternative proposal that is quite amazing and totally unexpected. Descartes takes this boastful and bizarre invention as a pretext to outline what according to him would be the definitive program for human beings regarding language: namely, a reasoned and systematic catalog of all infinite possible thoughts. The following are his words, and they contain an astonishing gem:

> Besides, I find it possible to add another invention to this, both for composing the primitive words of this language and for their characters, in such a way that it can be taught very quickly and by means of an order, that is to say, by establishing an order among all the thoughts that can enter the human mind, just as there is a natural order established among numbers. And just as in a single day one can learn to give names to all numbers up to infinity and to write them in an unknown language, even though they would amount to an infinite number of different words, one could do the same thing with all other necessary words to express all the other things that fall within the human mind. If this order were discovered, I have no doubt that this language would soon spread throughout the world, for many people would have the desire to spend five or six days in order to make themselves understood by all men.[2]

Before approaching the very core of this quotation, let's consider some important collateral aspects. Descartes is not the only one who dared dream of discovering a better or a perfect or universal or at least unambiguous language; shortly after him, in the same century, Gottfried Wilhelm Leibniz offered his *Lingua characteristica universalis* and Juan de Caramuel y Lobkowitz, bishop of Vigevano, his *Leptotatos*; jumping ahead to the twentieth century, Louis Hjelmslev presented his *Glossematics* and Giuseppe Peano his *Algebra de gramatica*. These efforts continued all the way to the great scam of ingenious and perfect languages that have sadly led to the delirium of a ranking among tongues and the effort to anchor them in the notion of "race."[3]

There is of course a danger to searching for a perfect language, and it is a danger that is not just fictitious since it was the aberrant link between an alleged perfect language and the human race that gave rise to the delirious notion of a group of humans superior to others. It started in the mid-twentieth century with the Bavarian-born linguist Max Müller's hypothesis that a noble language could be spoken only by people of the noble race, with the term "noble" standing in for "Aryan." He refuted his theory later in life, but by then it was too late: This delusional idea had already taken root in countries all over the world and fed the political propaganda of governments calling for aggression against other populations, and even extermination, as in the case of Jewish people. The fact that the notion of race is not biologically sustainable proved to be completely insufficient in preventing the social consequences of this delirium. In fact—one should not forget this—as humans, we still see average, shared phenotypical differences between groups of people—skin color, the shape of the eyes, or average height—and the necessity to name them emerges naturally, if not with the collective term *race*, which nowadays has negative connotations, then with other equivalent terms like *ethnicity*: the substance, based on our natural capacity to distinguish and to group like with like, remains the same, however biologically irrelevant it may be. But even if these biological details are eliminated on scientific grounds at the molecular level, since we know that the genomic difference between individuals of what we call the same race may be greater than the average one between what we call different races, another much more dangerous and underestimated issue remains on another level: cognition. In fact, two independent ideas that are not generally taken to be dangerous in isolation constitute a powerfully explosive mixture if considered together.

The first idea is the hypothesis that some languages are better than others. There is a notion that some languages have a lexicon that captures abstract concepts better than others, or that some languages operate more quickly than others, that some appear to have a more stable word order in their sentences while others have an unconstrained, even chaotic word order—that some languages are even just acoustically more pleasant or harmonic than others.

The second idea is the hypothesis that a person perceives reality and reasons about it differently depending on what language they speak.

These two hypotheses, regarded by many as being factual, ipso facto reproduce the most radical, dangerous, and pervasive of all racisms: the one that bears on a person's capacity to understand, think, and love. Interestingly, Dante, in his *De vulgari eloquentia*, already knew that this was a delusional argument. In fact, in the scholarly treatise on languages he wrote in Latin, he mocks those who think a "better" language is possible by referring to Pietramala, an abandoned small village or a crumbling manor on the Italian Apennines between Bologna and Firenze, where the Tarlatis, a family rival to the Alighieris, lived (not quite a city, let alone a great one): "Pietramala is a great city indeed, the home of the greater part of the children of Adam. For whoever is guided by such an *obscene* reasoning as to think that the place of his birth is the most delightful spot under the sun, he may also believe that his own language, i.e., his mother tongue, excels over all others; and, as a result, he may believe that his language was also Adam's language."[4]

In this passage Dante uses a very strong and aggressive adjective, "obscene" (in Latin *obscenus*, meaning both "indecent" and "inauspicious"), to qualify this reasoning—quite surprising for a high-end treatise devoted to intellectuals of all countries. This stylistic mark indirectly highlights Dante's strong feelings, if not outrage: By exploiting such a harsh irony and unexpected verbal crudity he expresses his opposition to those who conflate the affective domain with the rational one. Being in love with someone doesn't authorize the lover to argue that one's beloved is the best person in the world; the same holds for languages. Had Western culture listened and read Dante carefully—something that sadly didn't happen, as even Alessandro Manzoni recognized—we may have not engaged with the delirious notion of a noble language and a noble race. There is simply no language that is better than another—and certainly no perfect language.

That said, turning back to Descartes's reflections, his comparison of a natural order of thoughts to the natural order of numbers is astonishing, both for the force of his analysis and for its synthetic discussion. It arguably surpasses all other similar such dreamers in the history of Western thought: What would be needed is "an order among all the thoughts that can enter the human mind, just as there is a natural order established among numbers."[5] Some examples may clarify his intuition: No one ever doubts which number follows, say, the number called *one thousand seven hundred and twenty-two* and what its name is; but when it comes to which word *follows* the word *cloud*, no one knows, and this is necessarily the case. We can perhaps think of the plural *clouds*, and then *cloudy*, the adjective that is derived from it, but we know these only because in the alphabetical order another letter, *s*, is added to *cloud*, making *clouds* a successor of *cloud*, and *cloudy* a successor to *clouds* because *y* follows the *s*. But that pertains to the form, the signifier, the sound: when it come to a word's content, the signified or the meaning, we are just not capable of placing words into an exhaustive, complete natural order, one that is totally derivable from primitive elements. Such was the dream expressed by Descartes, or perhaps we should say *mirage*, but it is a very important dream for at least three reasons. The first is that everyone would like to have a map of meanings for knowing the borders of Babel—which would amount to having a map of *impossible meanings*. The second is that we would like to understand how words are stored in our brain; sometimes slips make us understand that they are in alphabetical order, leading us to mistakenly utter *bed* instead of *bread*, but other times they must be arranged according to meaning because we will mistakenly utter a conceptually contiguous noun *chair* instead of *bed*. The third is that today machines are being built that are capable of working on language in an automatic way; I am thinking of such popular "talking machines" as ChatGPT. These utilize a type of computational model involving "neural networks" or (very) large language models, referred to as "(v)LLMs," the latest in a series of inventions that started in the 1900s that then went by the now obsolete term "cybernetics" before getting renamed as "artificial intelligence." While AI is a fairly opaque name for this,[6] it is at least less pretentious than what gets referred to as "neuronal or neural networks," whose mechanisms remain quite mysterious, given what we know about neurons. As Gerald Edelman claimed, "perhaps the most important general observation that can be made about the brain is that its anatomy is the most important thing about it."[7]

None of these attempts can compete in ambition with the Cartesian dream of a natural order among word meanings, but there is substantial difference: The Cartesian dream suggests an opportunity to know language structure, our limits, and thus, ultimately, ourselves in a better way (witness Descartes's illuminating caveat "if this order were discovered"). On the other hand, modern research in technology aims to facilitate everyday life by creating machines that can help humans perform routine tasks. Ever since the invention of the first tool, we have designed artificial objects to help us avoid fatigue and boredom. One difference needs to be highlighted, though: To properly compare and contrast humans and machines, it is important to understand each one's intrinsic limits. It wasn't that long ago that we thought machines were too primitive to resemble humans and that we needed to wait for more advanced technology for them to be capable of doing what we do. Today, talking machines have led us to radically overturn this perspective and support the epoch-making strides of formal and comparative linguistics in the second half of the twentieth century. The central fact is quite easy to grasp, given what we've observed so far: for machines, there exist no impossible languages.[8] Actually, we need to be clear on this point: Even if a machine demonstrates a different "behavior" in how it understands an impossible language (the way humans do), the nonbiological nature of impossible languages still establishes a difference between humans and machines. Humans exploit natural circuits developed by genetic instructions under evolutionary forces, but only for possible languages; impossible languages progressively inhibit those circuits and are computed by other networks in the brain. In other words, for machines and their grammars (the vLLM-based programs), even the very notion of "natural circuit" has no empirical equivalent: Machines don't resemble us humans, not because they lack computational power, but because they are too powerful. Ultimately, they do not look like us because they do not have our limits: After all, we are our limits.

Of course, from a purely scientific point of view, an experiment is missing from all this—an impossible experiment for purely ethical reasons—which would consist in teaching children an artificial impossible language and studying the result. The experiment can obviously be carried out only on consenting adults. Luckily, science is still guided by a code of ethics, and this experiment remains, more or less as Descartes recommended, confined to the realm of novels such as in the one I attempted by writing *Il segreto di Pietramala* (*The Secret of Pietramala*), which sought to see through Umberto Eco's recommendation that "whereof one cannot theorize, thereof one must narrate."[9]

What stands out after this reading, at least to me, is that Lucretius's reflections on the alphabet as a model of the universe, and specifically on the permutation of the order of primitive elements as an essential factor of this model, should not be dismissed as an antiquarian discovery. The very idea of a grammar for the cosmos still stimulates us today, and it allows us, two thousand years later, to think about our limits, our understanding of the world and its connection with our brain, and, finally, to trace a meaningful, non-mystical, and in fact quite measurable and substantial border between humans and machines. We still have good reasons to read Lucretius and allow him to lead us to formulate the right questions about the real Big Bang that concerns us here—the big bang of language—because ultimately, when we reflect on language, the data we're considering is ourselves.

8 FEAR, REASON (AND HOPE)

Four times, in privileged sites of his poem (the *incipits* of the three pairs of books that make up *De Rerum Natura*, and in the sixth book), Lucretius praises Epicurus and presents him his infinite and devoted gratitude and, on his behalf, that of all humankind. Epicurus—Lucretius is explicit on this— saves us. Those years when Lucretius wrote his poem were special years for Western civilization: In the Roman empire of the first century BCE, the cathedral of pagan superstition, crowded with capricious deities representing the futility of human beings, had been practically dismantled, and the powerful wave of the Christian creed, a "reform" of the much older Jewish creed, was still to come, although it was— perhaps not accidentally, at least from a purely sociological point of view—imminent. In those years, Epicurus was an almost necessary anchor for those who didn't want to throw themselves at the mercy of nothingness: Never was the *horror vacui* so powerful and apparently inevitable as in those years. Lucretius, in his poem, wanted to promote the atomic explanation of the world Epicurus had derived from Democritus throughout the communities of intellectuals and scholars who spoke Latin—a community much larger than the small circle of Greek-speaking philosophers populating the ancient Roman Empire. His effort, however, was not manifested as a frigid didactic impulse or an erudite pedagogy; his text—like all self-respecting texts—has a positive function, one that offers change both in individuals' and society's lives. This goal is clear in many points of the poem, but perhaps more so when Lucretius addresses Epicurus and praises him with these words:

> For when your reason, which took structure from the divine mind,
>
> began to express the nature of things in words,
>
> then all fears fled.[1]

Then all fears fled: This is the concrete result on people's lives Lucretius anticipates from adopting Epicurus's philosophy intertwined with Democritus's physics. And ultimately, this is why Lucretius places Epicurus at the center of the poem, because it is Epicurus who, by resorting to reason, peeled the patina off from miraculous readings of reality that in the end only make individuals feel subjugated by fate and inevitable disappointment. And people were grateful to him; and we too are grateful to him, even if many of the patinas remain, sometimes hidden even behind the screen of a certain way of understanding science, such as the one that leads us to believe that we will understand everything one day, or the one that allows no opportunity to express one of the greatest statements freedom allows: "I don't know."

However, one thing regarding *De Rerum Natura* is clear. We don't know how Lucretius would have concluded his masterpiece; the majority of critics agree that it is an unfinished poem written during the breaks of his psychotic attacks recounted in ancient sources, perhaps due to an

aphrodisiac drug (*poculum amatorium*), that led him to sui-
cide.[2] We cannot be sure about these biographical details,
but we do know one thing: that his descriptions toward the
end of the poem—the description of the plague in Athens
in 430 BCE, the same one described by Thucydides in the
second book of the *Peloponnesian War*—evoke visceral fear
in the reader, contrasting with his own words: *Then all fears
fled.* If reason is to chase away all fears, either we have not
yet found sufficient rational tools to do away with the fear
of death—especially atrocious forms of death—or we have
yet to realize that the answer to this fear cannot be found in
ourselves alone. *Tertium non datur.*

I would rather not translate the lines in which Lucretius describes the plague (the passage can be found in *De
Rerum Natura* VI: 1138–1286): I have never read anything
more terrifying. To my mind, not even other major authors'
descriptions of the plague—Thucydides, followed by Soph-
ocles, Giovanni Boccaccio, Geoffrey Chaucer, Alessandro
Manzoni, Jack London, and Albert Camus—can compare
with Lucretius's text. Lucretius makes you feel the plague
growing inside you, as if it was the devil himself conjuring it
up; the harshest symptoms are described in such a realistic
way that they make your head spin and you feel the urge to
stop reading. The experience is also somewhat ironic since
the description of the plague is transmitted through nothing
but a permutation of the order of the letters of the alphabet
which are the tools that reason exploits to try to chase away
all fears by assuming an atomistic view of life and death.
Perhaps Lucretius wanted to put us to the test and show

what letters are capable of doing to us. Alternatively, we can imagine that Lucretius had a sensational ending to his poem in mind in which reason would be able to destroy this ultimate fear and dissolve it into a new awareness of reality and of ourselves. But let's stay with facts, and the text we have: What is clear is that understanding how a disease "works" evidently does not dispel the fear of that disease or of death, not even when it is a death that affects someone other than ourselves. And in the last book of *De Rerum Natura* we are eventually left with no escape in the face of this insurmountable wall of pain, unmoving before any act of reason, only to ask ourselves: Why isn't reason enough to chase our fears away? And what is it that we are afraid of? We could ask where fear itself comes from if everything is made up of a combination of elements that cannot feel anything. Clearly, Lucretius already warned us about the emergence of unexpected properties within this atomic view of the world.

I don't know, and I don't want to suggest to anyone a way out of this fearful, paradoxical and absurd situation, because it is the responsibility of every individual—be it on their own or in whom they choose to trust—to decide this crucial issue. Lucretius's ultimate message may have been precisely to encourage us to understand that we must learn to choose whom we entrust ourselves, which is after all the goal of any education; a need that was certainly vivid and valid in his disoriented times but even more so today, an era in which disorientation appears to be greater than ever. Moreover, for the first time in the history of humanity, it is more difficult to discard sources of information than it is to find them, which makes trusting someone necessary, given that it is literally impossible—I would say physically impossible—to fathom on our own all that is known and written. Here technology really does matter for humans.

But we will never know if this was the end he had envisaged for his poem. For me, what remains after reading this masterpiece is, along with an indefeasible fascination for a rational reading of the universe, a laceration that does not heal. The understanding that we are made of atoms, while true and compelling, does not exhaust our fundamental questions. I'm aware that I'm repeating myself, but I can't help pointing out the contrast I feel with the thought of a modern biologist, Jacques Monod, who at the end of his most famous book, *Chance and Necessity*, sings the hymn of joy that emerges for him from this awareness: "The ancient covenant is in pieces; man knows at last that he is alone in the universe's unfeeling immensity, out of which he emerged only by chance. His destiny is nowhere spelled out, nor is his duty. The kingdom above or the darkness below: it is for him to choose."[3] I can find no convincing rational arguments that choosing chance doesn't coincide with a first step into Darkness.

Lucretius's conclusion is a disconcerting, unexpected event: The fear that he makes us experience, described in the last verses of his masterpiece, confirms the force of reason but does so in a totally indirect, painful manner, and makes it clear that he must have performed the laceration he describes on himself. It does so because, while not denying reason even in the face of the abyss, he shows us that we have no alternative but to nourish hope; in fact, had he lost hope he wouldn't have wasted time writing for others. For this reason, we wish to believe that Lucretius wrote to us, as the first step toward the building of a cathedral that only future generations may inhabit, and because he did so, he continues to enlighten us, by simply permuting the order of letters.

I put the book back on the desk, picked up the glass of water, and drank it. It was cool: The ice had melted, hit by a ray of light.

> You must always be ready to give an explanation to everyone
>
> who asks you for the reason for the hope
>
> that is in you.
>
> —1 Peter 3:15

Acknowledgments

The seeds of this reflections do not come from me: they come from the impact of Lucretius's words. I first discovered this book when I was a boy and could not understand it; now that I am old I still can't understand, but its impact is greater. A sensation I can't just claim for myself alone: This decision would not have been taken without the encouragement of Marco Vigevani and Marc Lowenthal. I owe Marc a special thank you for his marvelous critical and stylistic work to render my notes to and translation of Lucretius's thought approachable. This book has also sharply benefited from the criticism and the suggestions of three anonymous reviewers. Reviewing has become a delicate issue nowadays and I can't but be grateful for their cooperative attitude as well as their effort to understand my intentions. Also a grateful thank you to Judith Feldmann for her special eye and sensitivity in digging out inconsistencies and stylistic awkwardness. Special thanks also to Elisabetta Sgarbi and Eugenio Lio for their intuition of a positive role of a "pop version" of this astonishing unparalleled poem, written by a genius *per intervalla insaniae*, during those unique years of our civilization when the Gods were dead and reason was not sufficient to survive the burden of fears. My wish is that sharing it will increase the desire to search for reasons for hope.

Notes

PROLOGUE

1. See I. Calvino, "Italiani, vi esorto ai classici," *L'Espresso*, June 28, 1981.

2. See A. Moro, *Impossible Languages* (Cambridge, MA: MIT Press, 2016).

PART I

1. As he stated in his 1874 essay, "The Limits of Our Knowledge of Nature," *Popular Science Monthly* 369 (1874): 17–32. For a critical discussion and an illustration of Émil du Bois-Reymond, see F. Vidoni, *Ignorabimus! Emil du Bois-Reymond e il dibattito sui limiti della conoscenza scientifica nell'Ottocento* (Milan: Marcos y Marcos, 1988) and G. Finkelstein, *Émil du Bois-Reymond: Neuroscience, Self and Society in Nineteenth-Century Germany* (Cambridge, MA: MIT Press, 2013).

2. Nunc locus est, ut opinor, in his illud quoque rebus

    confirmare tibi, nullam rem posse sua vi

    corpoream sursum ferri sursumque meare,

    ne tibi dent in eo flammarum corpora fraudem;

    sursus enim versus gignuntur et augmina sumunt,

    et sursum nitidae fruges arbustaque crescunt,

    pondera, quantum in se est, cum deorsum cuncta ferantur.

    nec cum subsiliunt ignes ad tecta domorum

    et celeri flamma degustant tigna trabesque,

sponte sua facere id sine vi subiecta putandum est.

quod genus e nostro cum missus corpore sanguis

emicat exultans alte spargitque cruorem.

nonne vides etiam quanta vi tigna trabesque

respuat umor aquae? nam quo magis ursimus altum

derecta et magna vi multi pressimus aegre,

tam cupide sursum revomit magis atque remittit,

plus ut parte foras emergant exiliantque.

nec tamen haec, quantum estinse, dubitamus, opinor,

quin vacuum per inane deorsum cuncta ferantur.

sic igitur debent quoque flammae posse per auras

aeris expressae sursum succedere, quamquam

pondera, quantum in sest, deorsum deducere pugnent.

(*DRN* II: 184–205)

3. For a historical and critical discussion of this issue, see J. Durham Peters, "Made Absolutely Exact: Borges and Royce on Maps and Media," *Variaciones Borges* 25 (2008): 1–23.

CHAPTER 1

1. ut potius multis communia corpora rebus

    multa putes esse, ut verbis elementa videmus,

    quam sine principiis ullam rem existere posse.

    (*DRN* I: 196–198)

2. atque eadem magni refert primordia saepe

    cum quibus et quali positura contineantur

    et quos inter se dent motus accipiantque;

    namque eadem caelum mare terras flumina solem

    constituunt, eadem fruges arbusta animantis,

verum aliis alioque modo commixta moventur.
quin etiam passim nostris in versibus ipsis
multa elementa vides multis communia verbis,
cum tamen inter se versus ac verba necessest
confiteare et re et sonitu distare sonanti.
tantum elementa queunt permutato ordine solo;
(*DRN* I: 816–827)

3.   iamne vides igitur, paulo quod diximus ante,
permagni referre eadem primordia saepe
cum quibus et quali positura contineantur
et quos inter se dent motus accipiantque,
atque eadem paulo inter se mutata creare
ignes et lignum? quo pacto verba quoque ipsa
inter se paulo mutatis sunt elementis,
cum *ligna* atque *ignes* distincta voce notemus.
(*DRN* I: 907–914)

4.   Quin etiam passim nostris in versibus ipsis
multa elementa vides multis communia verbis,
cum tamen inter se versus ac verba necesse est
confiteare alia ex aliis constare Elementis;
non quo multa parum communis littera currat
aut nulla inter se duo sint ex omnibus isdem,
sed quia non volgo paria omnibus omnia constant.
(*DRN* II: 688–694)

5.   quin etiam refert nostris in versibus ipsis
cum quibus et quali sint ordine quaeque locata;
namque eadem caelum mare terras flumina solem

significant, eadem fruges arbusta animantis;

si non omnia sunt, at multo maxima pars est

consimilis; verum positura discrepitant res.

sic ipsis *in* rebus item iam materiai

[intervals vias conexus pondera plagas]

concursus motus ordo positura figurae

cum permutantur, mutari res quoque debent.

(*DRN* II 1013–1022)

6. The story is well told by Stephen Greenblatt in *The Swerve: How the World Became Modern* (New York: W. W. Norton, 2011).

7. Ferdinand de Saussure, *Course in General Linguistics*, ed. Charles Bally and Albert Sechehaye, trans. Wade Baskin (New York: The Philosophical Library, 1959), 115.

8. See Noam Chomsky and Andrea Moro, *The Secrets of Words* (Cambridge, MA: MIT Press, 2022).

9. "τὰ μὲν στοιχεῖα ἄγνωστα, τὸ δὲ τῶν συλλαβῶν γένος γνωστόν . . . X ρῆν γὰρ ἴσως τὴν συλλαβὴν τίθεσθαι μὴ τὰ στοιχεῖα ἀλλ, ἐξ ἐκείνων ἕν τι γεγονὸς εἶδος, ἰδέαν μίαν αὐτὸ αὑτοῦ ἔχον, ἕτερον δὲ τῶν στοιχείων" (Thaet. 202e, 203b, 203d).

10. Perrin quoted in F. Jacob, *La Logique du vivant: Une histoire de l'hérédité* (Paris: Gallimard, 1974); trans. *The Logic of Life: A History of Heredity* (New York: Pantheon Books, 1979).

CHAPTER 2

1. nil esse, in promptu quorum natura videtur,

quod genere ex uno consistat principiorum,

nec quicquam quod non permixto semine constet.

(*DRN* II: 583–585)

2. . . . primordia rerum,

inter se simili quae sunt perfecta figura,

infinita cluere

(*DRN* II: 523–525)

3.   . . . primordia rerum

finita variare figurarum ratione.

(*DRN*: II 479–480)

4.   For the evolution of the notion of gravity from a nontechnical point of view, see R. Feynman, *The Character of the Physical Law* (Cambridge, MA: MIT Press, 1967). For an introduction to this idea of the graviton, see Reichenbach, *The Philosophy of Space and Time* (New York: Dover, 1951).

5.   contemplator enim, cum solis lumina cumque

inserti fundunt radii per opaca domorum:

multa minuta modis multis per inane videbis

corpora misceri radiorum lumine in ipso

et velut aeterno certamine proelia pugnas

edere turmatim certantia nec dare pausam,

conciliis et discidiis exercita crebris;

conicere ut possis ex hoc, primordia rerum

quale sit in magno iactari semper inani.

dumtaxat, rerum magnarum parva potest res

exemplare dare et vestigia notitiai.

(*DRN* II: 114–124)

6.   "Solida atque individua vi et gravitate ferri mundumque effici ornatissimum et pulcherrimum ex eorum corporum concursione fortuita? Hoc qui existimat fieri potuisse, non intellego cur non idem putet, si innumerabiles unius et viginti formae litterarum vel aureae vel qualislibet aliquo coiciantur, posse ex iis in terram excussis annales Ennii ut deinceps legi possint

effici; quod nescio an ne in uno quidem versu possit tantum valere fortuna" (*De Natura Deorum* II, 37w).

7. Fred Hoyle, *The Intelligent Universe* (New York: Holt, Rinehart, and Winston, 1984), 19.

8. For Oparin's thesis and related issues see Iris Fry, "The Origins of Research into the Origins of Life," *Endeavour* 30, no. 1 (2006): 24–28.

9. See his illuminating book: Erwin Schrödinger, *What Is Life? The Physical Aspect of the Living Cell* (Cambridge: Cambridge University Press, 1944).

10. On this question, see the discussion in Chomsky and Moro, *The Secrets of Words*, and the quotes contained therein, the one from Émil Du Bois-Reymond in particular. I also recommend Faustino Savoldi, Mauro Ceroni, and Luca Vanzago, *La Coscienza: Contributi per specialisti e non specialisti tra Neuroscienze, Filosofia e Neurologia* (Fano: Aras Edizioni, 2013); and Giorgio Vallortigara, *Pensieri di una mosca con la testa storta* (Milan: Adelphi, 2021).

11. Émile Bernard, *Souvenirs sur Paul Cézanne et lettres* (Paris: A la rénovation esthétique, 1948), 36.

12. Andrea Moro, *I Speak, Therefore I Am: Seventeen Thoughts About Language*, trans. Ian Roberts (New York: Columbia University Press, 2016), 12–13; new enlarged edition Milano Adelphi, 2024.

13. See Elena Castellani, "On the Meaning of Symmetry Breaking," in *Symmetries in Physics: Philosophical Reflections*, ed. Katherine Brading and Elena Castellani (Cambridge: Cambridge University Press, 2003), 321–334.

14. Alan Turing, "The Chemical Basis of Morphogenesis," *Philosophical Transactions of the Royal Society of London* 237, no. 641 (1952): 37–72.

15. To understand the role of symmetry breaking in human language syntax, see Andrea Moro, *Dynamic Antisymmetry:*

Movement as a Symmetry-Breaking Phenomenon (Cambridge, MA: MIT Press, 2000); and Andrea Moro and Ian Roberts, "The Duality of Syntax," *Natural Language & Linguistic Theory* 42 (2023): 609–631. For a less-technical illustration see Moro, *The Boundaries of Babel*, 2nd ed. (Cambridge, MA: MIT Press, 2015), or Moro, *Impossible Languages* (Cambridge, MA: MIT Press, 2016). A straightforward example of a symmetry-breaking phenomenon in human language can be found in phonology. Phonology is assumed to allow the combination of symmetrical items, such as sequences of vowels [VV], to depart from the most common asymmetrical [CV] structure combining a consonant with a vowel. Grammar provides a mechanism to restore asymmetry by inserting a consonant: [VCV]. This phenomenon is well known and is called *epenthesis*. In British English, for example, when a verbal root like *draw* is combined with the *-ing* suffix, the pronunciation of *drawing* includes the insertion between the two vowels of a so-called "intrusive r," yielding: /ˈdrɔː(r)ɪŋ/. The core idea of dynamic antisymmetry is that there is such a thing as "syntactic epenthesis" that avoids the combination of symmetrical syntactic items.

16. "Notes inédites de F. de Saussure," *Cahiers F. de Saussure* 12 (1954): 64.

CHAPTER 3

1. Ergo formarum novitatem corporis augmen
   subesquitur
   (*DRN* II: 495–496)

2. Huc accedit ut in summa res nulla sit una,
   unica quae gignatur et unica solaque crescat,
   quin aliquoiu' siet saecli permultaque eodem
   sint genere.
   (*DRN* II: 1076–1080)

3. Nunc age dicta meo dulci quaesita labore
   percipe, ne forte haec albis ex alba rearis
   principiis esse, ante oculos quae candida cernis,
   aut ea quae nigrant nigro de semine nata;
   nive alium quemvis quae sunt inbuta colorem,
   propterea gerere hunc credas, quod materiai
   corpora consimili sint eius tincta colore;
   nullus enim color est omnino materiai
   corporibus, neque par rebus neque denique dispar.
   (*DRN* II: 730–738)

4. See Giorgio Graffi, *200 Years of Syntax: A Critical Survey* (Amsterdam: John Benjamins, 2001).

5. See John Ries, *Was ist ein Satz* (Prague: Taussig & Taussig, 1927).

6. See A. Moro, *The Raising of Predicates: Predicative Noun Phrases and the Theory of Clause Structure* (Cambridge: Cambridge University Press, 1997), and A. Moro, *A Brief History of the Verb* To Be, trans. Bonnie McClellan-Broussard (Cambridge, MA: MIT Press, 2017).

7. See Andrea Moro, *A Brief History of the Verb* To Be, trans. Bonnie McClellan-Broussard (Cambridge, MA: MIT Press, 2017).

8. quod si delira haec furiosaque cernimus esse,
   et ridere potest non ex ridentibus auctus,
   et sapere et doctis rationem reddere dictis
   non ex seminibus sapientibus atque disertis,
   qui minus esse queant ea quae sentire videmus
   seminibus permixta carentibus undique sensu?
   (*DRN* II: 985–990)

9. The idea that certain properties emerge from coordination of elements that do not inherently have that property goes as far as today theories of consciousness. See, for example, S. Hameroff and R. Penrose, "Consciousness in the Universe: A Review of the 'Orch OR' Theory," *Physics of Life Reviews* 11, no. 1 (2014): 39–78. Personally, I would quite still adhere to a dualist (Neo-cartesian) attitude, insofar as hypotheses *non fingenda sunt.*

CHAPTER 4

1. tunc et amicitiem coeperunt iungere aventes

   finitimi inter se nec laedere nec violari,

   et pueros commendarunt muliebreque saeclum,

   vocibus et gestu cum balbe significarent

   imbecillorum esse aequum misererier omnis.

   (*DRN* V: 1019–1023)

2. See Andrea Moro, *La razza e la lingua: Sei lezioni sul razzismo* (Milan: La nave di Teseo, 2019), and *The Secret of Pietramala*, trans. Anne Milano Appel (Milan: La nave di Teseo, 2023). I will talk about the specific contribution of these two books later in the text.

3. The prevailing theory of the last ten years or so, that a prevailing function of sleep is to clean the brain from waste products and toxins, seems to be wrong. See Miao et al., "Brain Clearance Is Reduced During Sleep and Anesthesia," *Nature Neuroscience* 27 (2024): 1046–1050.

4. At varios linguae sonitus natura subegit

   mittere et utilitas expressit nomina rerum,

   non alia longe ratione atque ipsa videtur

   protrahere ad gestum pueros infantia linguae,

   cum facit ut digito quae sint praesentia monstrent.

sentit enim vim quisque suam quod possit abuti.
(*DRN* V: 1028–1033)

CHAPTER 5

1. Basing the reconstruction of the structure of language on the fact that it is also used to communicate (so-called inverse engineering) would be like reconstructing the structure of a foot from its use as a tool to walk. See M. Everaert et al., "What Is Language and How Could It Have Evolved?" *Trends in Cognitive Sciences* 21, no. 8 (2017): 569–571.

2. Hasce igitur penitus voces cum corpore nostro
   exprimimus rectoque foras emittimus ore,
   mobilis articulat verborum daedala lingua,
   formaturaque labrorum pro parte figurat.
   (*DRN* IV: 549–562)

3. See Moro, *Impossible Languages*.

4. cornua nata prius vitulo quam frontibus extent,
   illis iratus petit atque infestus inurget.
   at catuli pantherarum scymnique leonum
   unguibus ac pedibus iam tum morsuque repugnant,
   vix etiam cum sunt dentes unguesque creati.
   alituum porro genus alis omne videmus
   fidere et a pennis tremulum petere auxiliatum.
   (*DRN* V: 1034–1040)

5. Illud in his rebus vitium vehementer inesse
   effugere errorm vitareque praemetuenter,
   lumina ne facias oculorum clara creata,
   prospicere ut possimus, et ut proferre queamus

proceros passus, ideo fastigia posse
surarum ac feminum pedibus fundata plicari,
bracchia tum porro validas ex apta lacertis
esse manusque datas utraque [ex] parte ministras,
ut facere ad vitam possemus quae foret usus.
(*DRN* IV: 822–831)

6. cetera de genere hoc inter quae cumque pretantur,
omnia perversa praepostera sunt ratione,
nil ideo quoniam natumst in corpore ut uti
possemus, sed quod natumst id procreat usum.
nec fuit ante videre oculorum lumina nata,
nec dictis orare prius quam lingua creatast,
sed potius longe linguae praecessit origo
sermonem multoque creatae sunt prius aures
quam sonus est auditus, et omnia denique membra
ante fuere, ut opinor, eorum quam foret usus;
haud igitur potuere utendi crescere causa.
(*DRN* IV: 833–842)

7. See E. Mayr, *The Growth of Biological Thought* (Cambridge, MA: Belknap Press of Harvard University Press, 1982).

8. nec ratione docere ulla suadereque surdis,
quid sit opus facto, facilist; neque enim paterentur
nec ratione ulla sibi ferrent amplius auris
vocis inauditos sonitus obtundere frustra.
(*DRN* V: 1053–1055)

9. For an illustration of the role of pseudo-words in research on the biological foundations of language, see Moro, *Impossible Languages*.

10. See Moro, *Impossible Languages* and Moro, *I Speak Therefore I Am* for a short history of structuralist issues connected with the search of primitive elements.

11. Chomsky explicitly admits that this process applied to syntax followed the one applied to phonology (Chomsky, *Lectures on Government and Binding* [Dordrecht: Foris, 1981]); a similar path was tempted in semantics by Hjelmslev within the so called "glossematic" school (L. Hjelmslev, *Omkring sprogteoriens grundlæggelse: Festskrift udg. af Københavns Universitet* [Denmark, 1943]). Unfortunately, the latter approach could not quite arrive to a completion. See Moro, *I Speak Therefore I Am*, and Chomsky and Moro, *The Secrets of Words*, for a critical view, crucially comparing these attempts to AI large language models.

12. Eric Lenneberg, *Biological Foundations of Language* (New York: Wiley, 1967), 2.

13. For more technical information concerning Broca's area activity, see chapter 1 of Kandel et al., *Principles of Neural Science*, 5th ed. (New York: McGrawHill Medical, 2012). See also Cappa et al., "Broca's Aphasia, Broca's Area and Syntax: A Complex Relationship," *Behavioral and Brain Sciences* 23 (2000): 27–28; G. Ojeman et al., "Cortical Language Localization in Left, Dominant Hemisphere: An Electrical Stimulation Mapping Investigation in 117 Patients," *Journal of Neurosurgery* 71, no. 3 (1989): 316–326.

14. See Moro, *The Secret of Pietramala* (and Moro, *Impossible Languages*, for a more extensive argument). See also Chomsky and Moro, *The Secrets of Words*; for a summary of Chomsky's view on language, see N. Chomsky, "Genuine Explanations," in *Rich Descriptions and Simple Explanations in Morphosyntax and Language Acquisition: In Honor of Luigi Rizzi*, ed. G. Bocci, D. Botteri, C. Manetti, and V. Moscati (Oxford: Oxford University Press, 2024) and "The Miracle Creed and SMT" in *A Cartesian Dream*, for further comments.

As for the origins of the generative enterprise and its connection with the Western tradition, and one that contains all the seeds that were expressed in the "generative enterprise," see Chomsky's *Cartesian Linguistics: A Chapter in the History of Rationalist Thought*, 3rd ed. (Cambridge: Cambridge University Press, 2009).

15. unde refert nobis victor quid possit oriri,

    quid nequeat, finita potestas denique cuique

    quanam sit ratione atque alte terminus haerens.

    (*DRN* I: 75–77)

16. For a discussion on the force of explanation in linguistics as a theory of limits, see Chomsky, "Genuine Explanations"; Chomsky, "The Miracle Creed and SMT"; and Chomsky and Moro, *The Secrets of Words*.

17. See G. Longobardi et al., "Toward a Syntactic Phylogeny of Modern Indo-European Languages," *Journal of Historical Linguistics* 3, no. 1 (2013): 122–152.

18. See M. Mancini, "Il paradosso darwiniano: Convergenze e divergenze di paradigma," in *Sull'origine del linguaggio e delle lingue storico-naturali: Un confronto fra linguisti e non linguisti*, ed. E. Banfi (Rome: Bulzoni, 2013), 105–142; Lorenzo Tomasin, *Il caos e l'ordine* (Turin: Einaudi, 2019).

19. ergo si varii sensus animalia cogunt

    muta tamen cum sint, varias emittere voces,

    quanto mortalis magis aequumst tum potuisse

    dissimilis alia atque alia res voice notare!

    (*DRN* V: 1087–1090)

20. As for the fact that there are not even Mendelian-compatible phenomena between languages, see A. Moro, *The Boundaries of Babel*, 2nd ed. (Cambridge, MA: MIT Press, 2015). The idea is that until we find a trait with the typical distribution

of Mendelian genetics we cannot even begin the search for an alleged "gene of language." In fact, it could even be that what we call language is similar to the well-known Kanisza triangle, something that is not there but that we perceive as existing given the way we perceive the contours of independent elements. From this perspective, language itself would be not a "real object" but rather the result of something we combine out of elements. Similar considerations arise for other domains, as when we see constellations. There are just stars; the constellation are a somewhat instinctive product of our observation. Our language, then, could be a "Kanisza constellation," so to speak.

21. proinde putare aliquem tum nomina distribuiesse
rebus et inde homines didicisse vocabula prima,
desiperest. nam cur hic posset cuncta notare
vocibus et varios sonitus emittere linguae,
tempore eodem alii facere id non quisse putentur?
(*DRN* V: 1041–1045)

22. praeterea si non alii quoque vocibus usi
inter se fuerant, unde insita notities est
utilitatis et unde data est huic prima potestas,
quid vellet facere ut sciret animoque videret?
cogere item pluris unus victosque domare
non poterat, rerum ut perdiscere nomina vellent.
(*DRN* V: 1046–1051)

23. From *The New Science*, trans. Thomas Goddard Bergin and Max Harold Fisch, vol. I, sections II, LVII, and LX, first and second paragraphs (Ithaca, NY: Cornell University Press, 1948).

24. See Tomasin, *Il caos e l'ordine*.

CHAPTER 6

1. See K. Sears et al., "Development of Bat Flight: Morphologic and Molecular Evolution of Bat Wing Digits," *PNAS* 103, no. 17 (2006): 6581–6586.

2. See Eiberg et al., "Blue Eye Color in Humans May Be Caused by a Perfectly Associated Founder Mutation in a Regulatory Element Located within the HERC2 Gene Inhibiting OCA2 Expression," *Human Genetics* 123 (2008): 177–187, https://doi.org/10.1007/s00439-007-0460.

3. See R. C. Lewontin, "The Apportionment of Human Diversity," *Evolutionary Biology* 6 (1972): 381–398; E. Mayr, *The Growth of Biological Thought* (Cambridge, MA: Belknap Press of Harvard University Press, 1982); S. J. Gould, *The Structure of Evolutionary Theory* (Cambridge, MA: Belknap Press of Harvard University Press, 2002); A. Moro, "Kataptation or the QWERTY-Effect in Language Evolution," *Frontiers in Psychology* 2, no. 50 (2011).

4. See M. Gagliano, M. Renton, N. Duvdevani, M. Timmins, and S. Mancuso, "Out of Sight but Not Out of Mind: Alternative Means of Communication in Plants," *PLOS One* 7, no. 5 (2012): e37382.

5. See J.-P. Changeux, P. Courrège, and D. Danchin, "A Theory of the Epigenesis of Neuronal Networks by Selective Stabilization of Synapses," *PNAS* 70, no. 10 (1973): 2974–2978; J. Mehler, J. "Connaître par Désapprentissage," in *L'Unité de L'Homme*, ed. M. Piattelli- Palmarini and E. Morin (Paris: Le Seuil, 1974), 287–299; M. Piattelli-Palmarini, "Evolution, Selection and Cognition: From 'Learning' to Parameter Setting in Biology and the Study of Language," *Cognition* 31 (1989): 1–44; R. A. Thompson and C. A. Nelson, "Developmental Science and the Media: Early Brain Development," *American Psychologist* 56 (2001): 5–15; R. Berwick and N. Chomsky, *Why Only Us?* (Cambridge, MA: MIT Press, 2015).

6. N. Jerne, "The Generative Grammar of the Immune System," *Science* 229 (1985): 1057–1059.

7. V. Volterra, "Variazioni e fluttuazioni del numero d'individui in specie animali conviventi," *Membro dell'Accademia dei Lincei* 2 (1926), 31–113.

8. As conjectured in A. Moro, *La razza e la lingua: Sei lezioni sul razzismo* (Milan: La nave di Teseo, 2019).

9. Interestingly, the discovery that all bodies fall at the same speed was not made by means of a physical experiment but by means of a mental one by Galileo in his 1638 book *Discourses and Mathematical Demonstrations Relating to Two New Sciences*. In a nutshell, here's the reasoning formulated in the first day of the dialogue: To assume that a lighter sphere falls slower than a heavier sphere of the same dimensions leads to a paradox. If that were true, then when the two spheres are joined together and dropped, the lighter one would be slower the heavier one, but since they are joined they are even heavier than the heavier one. So, the only reasonable hypothesis is that each of them falls to the ground with equal speed. Apart from the empirical significance of this conclusion, it is extremely interesting from an evolutionary cognitive perspective: Although the human mind is endowed with the false instinctive belief that heavier objects fall faster than lighter ones, it nevertheless allows humans to grasp the real phenomenon in play, however counterintuitive it may be. It is also interesting to note that this reasoning, which is available to everyone, occurred—to the best of our knowledge—only to Galileo, about two thousand years after physics was born in ancient Greece. I am indebted to Owen Gingerich for pointing out the mental nature of Galileo's experiment to me.

CHAPTER 7

1. For the history of the alphabet, see M. Mancini, "Studi di Capitoli di grafemica altomedioevale: L'onomastica alfabetica e

i trattati *de litteris*," in *Un accademico impaziente: Studi in onore di Glauco Sanga*, ed. Gianluca Ligi, Giovanni Pedrini, and Franca Tamisari (Alessandria: Edizioni dell'Orso, 2018), and references cited therein; on the reason why the order of the alphabet changed with mechanical typewriters, see Andrea Moro, "*Kataptation* or the *QWERTY*-Effect in Language Evolution," *Frontiers in Psychology* 2, no. 50 (2011), https://doi.org/10.3389/fpsyg.2011.00050.

2. R. Descartes, "Lettre de Descartes a Mersenne," in *Ouvres de Descartes: Correspondence: Avril 1622–1638*, vol. I, edited by A.-P. Tannery and L. Cerf (Paris, 1897), 498–502. This letter has not received much attention despite its immense value, as I believe. I also comment on it in the appendix to Moro, *La razza e la lingua*.

3. The literature on these invented languages is abundant; see Umberto Eco, *La ricerca della lingua perfetta* (Oxford: Blackwell, [1993] 1995) and his cited references; for a version that also touches on the neurological and ethical aspects of this theme, see Moro, *La razza e la lingua* and references cited there, as well as Moro, *I Speak Therefore I Am*. On Caramuel, see J. Leptotatos Caramuel, *Latine subtilissimus* (Vigevano: Typis Episcopalibus, Camillo Conrado, 1681). On Peano, see G. Peano, "Algebra de Grammatica," *Schola et Vita* 5 (1930): 323–336. On Hjelmslev and glossematics, see Hjelmslev, *Omkring sprogteoriens grundlæggelse*, for a foundational view. The reader can also find a fictionalized version of this theme of perfect and impossible languages in my novel *The Secret of Pietramala*.

4. Dante, *De Vul. Eloq.* book I; I–VI.

5. The fact that numbers, in fact integers, have a predictable order doesn't mean that every subsect of integers is totally predictable. For example, there is no function that is able to generate all and only prime numbers. In fact, this is even more interesting, since there is no phenomenon that follows from

a law that contains all and only prime numbers, nor is there a phenomenon that shows patterns that can be related to all and only prime numbers: see J. Derbyshire, *Prime Obsession: Bernhard Riemann and the Greatest Unsolved Problem of Mathematics* (Washington, DC: Joseph Henry Press, 2003), and references cited there. For an invented grammar which follows patterns with primes, see Moro, *The Secret of Pietramala*.

6. The word "intelligence" actually raises a distinct problem of translation. In English, there is an ambiguity between the as yet undefined human capacity to exhibit a skill or apply knowledge and the capacity to obtain information. In fact, if by "artificial intelligence" we mean the latter definition, the concept is quite clear. But in many languages, the equivalent of *intelligence*, such as the Italian *intelligenza* or the French *intelligence*, has only the former definition, and since it is practically undefined it makes the expanded label "artificial intelligence" difficult to grasp in an unambiguous way.

7. See Gerald Edelman, "Building a Picture of the Brain," in *The Brain*, ed. G. Edelman and J.-P. Changeux (New Brunswick, NJ: Transactions Publishers, 2001), 37–70. See also Hameroff and Penrose, "Consciousness in the Universe," for the delicate issues of the role of microtubule in neuronal computation.

8. See Andrea Moro, "Embodied Syntax: Impossible Languages and the Irreducible Difference Between Humans and Machines," *Sistemi Intelligenti* 35, no. 2 (August 2023): 321–327; Andrea Moro et al., "Large Languages, Impossible Languages and Human Brains," *Cortex* 167 (2023): 82–85; M. Greco et al., "False Perspectives on Human Language: Why Statistics Needs Linguistics," *Frontiers in Language Sciences* 2 (2023): 1178932; J. Bolhuis et al., "Three Reasons Why AI Doesn't Model Human Language," *Nature* 627 (2024): 489.

9. U. Eco, *Umberto Eco in His Own Words*, edited by T. Thellefsen and B. Sorensen (Berlin: De Gruyter Mouton, 2017), 165.

This book is a thriller that contains hidden quotations from examples in Western literature, which show how important and constant this issue has been across centuries, cultures, and countries.

CHAPTER 8

1. nam simul ac ratio tua coepit vociferari

   naturam rerum, divina mente coortam,

   diffugiunt animi terrores,

   (*DRN* III: 14–16).

2. We know this fact from Saint Jerome's *Chronicon omnimondae historiae*: "Titus Lucretius poeta nascitur, qui postea amatorio poculo in furorem versus, cum aliquot libros per intervalla insaniae conscripsisset, quos postea Cicero emendavit, propria se manu interfecit, anno aetatis 44." In English: "The poet Titus Lucretius is born. He later turns to fury with an aphrodisiac, after having written several books during intervals of insanity, which Cicero later edited. He killed himself with his own hand, at the age of 44." The citation is quoted from Eusebius Pamphilus, *Chronici canones, Latine vertit, adauxit, ad sua tempora produxit S. Eusebius Hieronymus*, edited by John Knight Fotheringham (University of Oxford, 1923).

3. J. Monod, *Chance and Necessity: An Essay on the Natural Philosophy of Modern Biology* (New York: Vintage, 1972), 112.

Bibliography

The text of *De Rerum Natura* on which I relied is the second Oxoniense critical edition released in 1921, edited by Cyril Bayley. For the commentary, however, I mainly referred to the edition edited by Alessandro Schiesaro and translated by Renata Raccanelli, published by Einaudi in 2023, and the one edited by Ivano Dionigi and translated by Luca Canali, published by Rizzoli in 2000, as well as that of Bayley in the Oxoniense edition in three volumes and the second edition by Martin Ferguson Smith released in 1982 for the Loeb Classical Library. The translations of the quotations, both by Lucretius and by other authors, are mine, although I of course compared them to those already available. I have always tried to adhere to the text without striving to maintain the metric and poetic qualities of *De Rerum Natura*: They are extremely important, but I could not aim at restituting these faithfully, since they are rooted in sound and rhythm. All errors are, of course, my responsibility.

Atlan, H. *Entre le cristal e la fumée: essai sur l'organisation du vivant*. Paris: Éditions du Seuil, 1979.

Bailey, C. *Titi Lucreti De Rerum Natura*. 3 vols. Oxford: Clarendon Press, 1947.

Bernard, E. *Souvenirs sur Paul Cézanne et lettres*. Paris: A la rénovation esthétique, Quai de Bourbon, 1948.

Berwick, R., and N. Chomsky. *Why Only Us?* Cambridge, MA: MIT Press, 2015.

Bois Reymond, E. du. "The Limits of Our Knowledge of Nature." *Popular Science Monthly* 369 (1874): 17–32.

Bolhuis, J., S. Crain, S. Fong, and A. Moro. "Three Reasons Why AI Doesn't Model Human Language." *Nature* 627 (2024): 489.

Calvino, I. "Italiani, vi esorto ai classici." *L'Espresso*, June 28, 1981. Republished in I. Calvino *Perché leggere i classici*. Milan: Oscar Mondadori, 1991.

Cappa, S. F., A. Moro, D. Perani, and M. Piattelli-Palmarini. "Broca's Aphasia, Broca's Area and Syntax: A Complex Relationship." *Behavioral and Brain Sciences* 23 (2000): 27–28.

Caramuel, J. Leptotatos. *Latine subtilissimus*. Vigevano: Typis Episcopalibus, Camillo Conrado, 1681.

Castellani, E. "On the Meaning of Symmetry-Breaking." In *Symmetries in Physics: Philosophical Reflections*, edited by Brading–Castellani, 321–334. Cambridge: Cambridge University Press, 2003.

Changeux, J.-P., P. Courrège, and D. Danchin. "A Theory of the Epigenesis of Neuronal Networks by Selective Stabilization of Synapses." *PNAS* 70, no. 10 (1973): 2974–2978.

Chomsky, N. *Cartesian Linguistics: A Chapter in the History of Rationalist Thought*, 3rd ed. Cambridge: Cambridge University Press, 2009. (Originally published 1966.)

Chomsky, N. "Genuine Explanations." In *Rich Descriptions and Simple Explanations in Morphosyntax and Language Acquisition: In Honor of Luigi Rizzi*, edited by B. Bocci, D. Botteri, C. Manetti, and V. Moscati. Oxford: Oxford University Press, 2024.

Chomsky, N. *Lectures on Government and Binding*. Dordrecht: Foris, 1981.

Chomsky, N. "Minimalism: Where Are We Now, And Where Can We Hope to Go." 言語研究 (Gengo Kenkyu) 160 (2021): 1–41.

Chomsky, N. "The Miracle Creed and SMT." In *A Cartesian Dream: A Geometrical Account of Syntax; In Honor of Andrea Moro*, edited by M. Greco and D. Mocci. Brno: Lingbuzz Press, 2024.

Chomsky, N., and A. Moro. *The Secrets of Words*. Cambridge, MA: MIT Press, 2022.

Cicero [Marcus Tullius Cicero]. *Cicero: De Natura Deorum Liber I*, edited by A. Dyck. Cambridge: Cambridge University Press, 2003.

Descartes, R. "Lettre de Descartes a Mersenne." In *Ouvres de Descartes: Correspondence: Avril 1622–1638*, vol. I, edited by A.-P. Tannery and L. Cerf, 498–502. Paris, 1897.

Durham Peters, J. "Made Absolutely Exact: Borges and Royce on Maps and Media." *Variaciones Borges*, no. 25 (2008): 1–23.

Eco, U. *La ricerca della lingua perfetta*. Bari: Laterza, 1993. Translated by James Fentress as *The Search for the Perfect Language*. Cambridge: Blackwell, 1995.

Eco, U. *Umberto Eco in His Own Words*. Edited by T. Thellefsen and B. Sorensen. Berlin: De Gruyter Mouton, 2017.

Edelman, G. "Building a Picture of the Brain." In *The Brain*, edited by G. Edelman and J.-P. Changeux, 37–70. New Brunswick, NJ: Transaction Publishers, 2001.

Eiberg, H., J. Troelsen, M. Nielsen, et al. "Blue Eye Color in Humans May Be Caused by a Perfectly Associated Founder Mutation in a Regulatory Element Located Within the HERC2 Gene Inhibiting OCA2 Expression." *Human Genetics* 123 (2008): 177–187.

Eusebius Pamphilus. *Chronici canones, Latine vertit, adauxit, ad sua tempora produxit S. Eusebius Hieronymus.* Edited by John Knight Fotheringham. University of Oxford, 1923.

Everaert, M., M. Huybregts, R. Berwick, N. Chomsky, I. Tattersall, A. Moro, and J. J. Boluhis. "What Is Language and How Could It Have Evolved?" *Trends in Cognitive Sciences* 21, no. 8 (2017): 569–571.

Feynman, R. *The Character of the Physical Law*. Cambridge, MA: MIT Press, 1967. (Originally published in 1965.)

Finkelstein, G. *Emil du Bois-Reymond: Neuroscience, Self and Society in Nineteen-Century Germany*. Cambridge, MA: MIT Press, 2013.

Fry, I. "The Origins of Research into the Origins of Life." *Endeavour* 30, no. 1 (2006): 24–28.

Gagliano, M., M. Renton, N. Duvdevani, M. Timmins, and S. Mancuso. "Out of Sight but Not out of Mind: Alternative Means of Communication in Plants." *PLOS One* 7, no. 5 (2012): e37382.

Galilei, Galileo. *Dialogo sopra i due massimi sistemi del mondo tolemaico e copernicano*. Edited by G. B. Landini. Florence, 1632. Translated as *Dialogue Concerning the Two Chief World Systems: Ptolemaic and Copernican*, ed. S. Drake (New York: Modern Library, 2001).

Galileo Galilei. *Discorsi e dimostrazioni matematiche intorno a due nuove scienze*. Leiden, Holland, 1638. Translated by Henry Crew and A. de Salvio as *Dialogues Concerning Two New Sciences* (New York: Dover, 1954).

Gould, S. J. *The Structure of Evolutionary Theory*. Cambridge, MA: Belknap Press of Harvard University Press, 2002.

Graffi, G. *200 Years of Syntax: A Critical Survey*. Amsterdam: John Benjamins, 2001.

Greco, M., A. Cometa, F. Artoni, F. Robert, and A. Moro. "False Perspectives on Human Language: Why Statistics Needs Linguistics." *Frontiers in Language Sciences* 2 (2023): 1178932.

Greenberg, J. H., ed. *Universals of Language*. Cambridge, MA: MIT Press, 1963.

Greenblatt, S. *The Swerve: How the World Became Modern*. New York: W. W. Norton, 2012.

Hameroff, S., and R. Penrose. "Consciousness in the Universe: A Review of the 'Orch OR' Theory." *Physics of Life Reviews* 11, no. 1 (2014): 39–78.

Hjelmslev, L. *Omkring sprogteoriens grundlæggelse: Festskrift udg. af Københavns Universitet*. Denmark, 1943.

Jacob, F. *La Logique du vivant: Une histoire de l'hérédité*. Paris: Gallimard, 1974. Translated as *The Logic of Life: A History of Heredity* (New York: Pantheon Books, 1979).

Jerne, N. "The Generative Grammar of the Immune System." *Science* 229 (1985): 1057–1059.

Kandel, E., J. Schwartz, T. Jessell, S. Siegelbaum, and A. Hudspeth. *Principles of Neural Science.* 5th ed. New York: McGrawHill Medical, 2012.

Kanizsa, G. *Essays on Gestalt Perception.* New York: Praeger, 1979.

Lenneberg, E. *Biological Foundations of Language.* New York: Wiley, 1967.

Lewontin, R. C. "The Apportionment of Human Diversity." *Evolutionary Biology* 6 (1972): 381–398.

Longobardi, G., C. Guardiano, G. Silvestri, A. Boattini, and A. Ceolin. "Toward a Syntactic Phylogeny of Modern Indo-European Languages." *Journal of Historical Linguistics* 3, no. 1 (2013): 122–152.

Lucretius [Titus Lucretius Carus]. *Lucretii De Rerum Natura Libri Sex.* Edited by Cyril Bayley. Oxford: Oxford University Press, [1898] 1921.

Mancini, M. "Il paradosso darwiniano: Convergenze e divergenze di paradigma." In *Sull'origine del linguaggio e delle lingue storico-naturali: Un confronto fra linguisti e non linguisti,* ed. E. Banfi, 105–142. Rome: Bulzoni, 2013.

Mancini, M. "Studi di Capitoli di grafemica altomedioevale: L'onomastica alfabetica e i trattati *de litteris.*" In *Un accademico impaziente: Studi in onore di Glauco Sanga,* edited by G. Ligi, G. Pedrini, and F. Tamisari. Alessandria: Edizioni dell'Orso, 2018.

Mayr, E. *The Growth of Biological Thought.* Cambridge, MA: Belknap Press of Harvard University Press, 1982.

Mehler, J. "Connaître par Désapprentissage." In *L'Unité de L'Homme,* ed. M. Piattelli-Palmarini and E. Morin, 287–299. Paris: Le Seuil, 1974.

Miao, A., T. Luo, G. Hsieh, et al. "Brain Clearance Is Reduced During Sleep and Anesthesia." *Nature Neuroscience* 27 (2024): 1046–1050.

Monod, J. *Le Hasard et la Necessite—Essai sur la philosophie naturelle de la biologie moderne.* Paris: Éditions du Seuil, 1970. Translated by Austryn Wainhouse as *Chance and Necessity: An*

Essay on the Natural Philosophy of Modern Biology (New York: Vintage, 1972).

Moro, A. *The Boundaries of Babel*. 2nd ed. Cambridge, MA: MIT Press, 2015.

Moro, A. *A Brief History of the Verb* To Be. Trans. Bonnie McClellan-Broussard. Cambridge, MA: MIT Press, 2017.

Moro, A. *Dynamic Antisymmetry: Movement as a Symmetry-Breaking Phenomenon*. Cambridge, MA: MIT Press, 2000.

Moro, A. "Embodied Syntax: Impossible Languages and the Irreducible Difference Between Humans and Machines." *Sistemi Intelligenti* 35, no. 2 (August 2023): 321–327.

Moro, A. *Impossible Languages*. Cambridge, MA: MIT Press, 2016.

Moro, A. *I Speak Therefore I Am: 17 Snapshots on the Language*. 2nd enlarged ed. Milan: Adelphi, 2024. Translation of the first 2012 edition by Ian Roberts as *I Speak, Therefore I Am: Seventeen Thoughts About Language* (New York: Columbia University Press, 2016).

Moro, A. "*Kataptation* or the *QWERTY*-Effect in Language Evolution." *Frontiers in Psychology* 2, no. 50 (2011). https://doi.org/10.3389/fpsyg.2011.00050.

Moro, A. *La razza e la lingua: Sei lezioni sul razzismo*. Milan: La nave di Teseo, 2019.

Moro, A. *The Raising of Predicates: Predicative Noun Phrases and the Theory of Clause Structure*. Cambridge: Cambridge University Press, 1997.

Moro, A. *The Secret of Pietramala*. Trans. Anne Appel. Milan: La nave di Teseo, 2023.

Moro, A., M. Greco, and S. Cappa. "Large Languages, Impossible Languages and Human Brains." *Cortex* 167 (2023): 82–85.

Moro, A., and I. Roberts. "The Duality of Syntax." *Natural Language & Linguistic Theory* 42 (2023): 609–631. https://doi.org/10.1007/s11049-023-09588-z.

Ojemann, G., J. Ojemann, E. Lettich, and M. Berger. "Cortical Language Localization in Left, Dominant Hemisphere: An Electrical Stimulation Mapping Investigation in 117 Patients." *Journal of Neurosurgery* 71, no. 3 (1989): 316–326.

Peano, G. "Algebra de Grammatica." *Schola et Vita* 5 (1930): 323–336.

Piattelli-Palmarini, M. "Evolution, Selection and Cognition: From 'Learning' to Parameter Setting in Biology and the Study of Language." *Cognition* 31 (1989): 1–44.

Reichenbach, H. *The Philosophy of Space and Time.* New York: Dover, 1951.

Reinhardt, T. "Epicurus and Lucretius on the Origins of Language." *Classical Quarterly* 58, no. 1 (2008): 127–140.

Ries, J. *Was ist ein Satz.* Prague: Taussig & Taussig, 1927.

Savoldi, F., M. Ceroni, and L. Vanzago. *Conscience: Contributions for Specialists and Non-Specialists in Neuroscience, Philosophy and Neurology.* Fano: Aras Edizioni, 2013.

Schrödinger, E. *What Is Life? The Physical Aspect of the Living Cell.* Cambridge: Cambridge University Press, 1944.

Sears, K., R. R. Behringer, J. J. Rasweiler IV, and L. A. Niswander. "Development of Bat Flight: Morphologic and Molecular Evolution of Bat Wing Digits." *PNAS* 103, no. 17 (2006): 6581–6586.

Thompson, R. A., and C. A. Nelson. "Developmental Science and the Media: Early Brain Development." *American Psychologist* 56 (2001): 5–15.

Tomasin, L. *Il caos e l'ordine.* Turin: Einaudi, 2019.

Turing, A. M. "The Chemical Basis of Morphogenesis." *Philosophical Transactions of the Royal Society of London* 237, no. 641 (1952): 37–72.

Turing, A. M. "Computing Machinery and Intelligence." *Mind* 59 (1950): 433–460.

Vallortigara, G. *Pensieri di una mosca con la testa storta*. Milan: Adelphi, 2021.

Vico, G. *The New Science*. Tans. Thomas Goddard Bergin and Max Harold Fisch. In G. Vico, *Works*, edited by A. Battistini. Milan: Mondadori, [1744] 2005.

Vidoni, F. *Ignorabimus! Emil du Bois-Reymond e il dibattito sui limiti della conoscenza scientifica nell'Ottocento*. Milan: Marcos y Marcos, 1988.

Volterra, V. "Variazioni e fluttuazioni del numero d'individui in specie animali conviventi." *Membro dell'Accademia dei Lincei* 2 (1926): 31–113.

Publisher contact:
The MIT Press
Massachusetts Institute of Technology
77 Massachusetts Avenue, Cambridge, MA 02139
mitpress.mit.edu

EU Authorised Representative:
Easy Access System Europe, Mustamäe tee 50,
10621 Tallinn, Estonia
gpsr.requests@easproject.com

Printed by Integrated Books International,
United States of America